Improving Your
Selling
Know-How

Sophie
de Menthon

KOGAN PAGE

■NETWORK

Kogan Page is the UK member of the Euro Business Publishing Network.
The European members are:
Les Editions d'Organisation, France; Verlag Moderne Industrie, Germany;
Liber, Sweden; Franco Angeli, Italy; and Deusto, Spain.
The Network has been established in response to the growing demand for
international business information and to make the work of Network authors
available in other European languages.

Les Editions d'Organisation, 1992
Translated by Ann Leonard
Illustrated by Sool Sbiera

First published in France in 1992 by
Les Editions d'Organisation, 26 avenue Emile-Zola, 75015 Paris,
entitled Vous et .... Votre Savoir-Vendre, ISBN 2-7081-1467-0

This edition first published in Great Britain in 1993 by
Kogan Page Ltd, 120 Pentonville Road, London N1 9JN.

British Library Cataloguing in Publication Data.
A CIP record for this book is available from the British Library.

ISBN 0 7494 1046 9

DTP for Kogan Page by
Jeff Carter 197 South Croxted Road, London SE21 8AY

Printed in Great Britain by
Biddles Ltd, Guildford and Kings Lynn

TABLE OF CONTENTS

The following symbols are used throughout this book to indicate:

 Find your way.

 Fill it in.

Case Study
SELLING – REDEEMED AT LAST

Commerce and negotiation have been the basis of all civilizations but the role of intermediary has been regarded, depending on the situation, as honourable or dishonourable, respected or derided.

After the Second World War the reputation of selling was stripped of all prestige. A world shortage of manufactured goods meant that little or no skill was required to sell anything and the balance was only redressed when supply eventually outstripped demand.

Advertising became the supreme communicator, presenting a flattering image of both consumer and manufacturer. Sales people, however, were often looked down upon; in certain circles they pretended they were not selling and merely making social calls during which an order or enquiry might surface. Many inexperienced sales people were recruited and no training was given. They did not enhance the reputation of their calling. But inefficient businesses were in for a rude awakening.

The communication sector realized it had not incorporated in its luring jingles the chords which actually struck home, and had ignored opportunities for direct contact with the customer, such as mail shots, reply-paid coupons, telesales, after-sales service and follow-up. It had been so enraptured with public relations to seduce the public that it had overlooked the main purpose of the exercise: to sell!

The development of consumerism has forced businesses to consider the client's needs and to accompany the client through every stage of the buying process, even to the extent of knowing how to dispose of the purchase when its useful life is over.

The consumer is no longer content simply to window-shop, whether it be as a result of something he's seen in a magazine, on the television or around him in his daily life. He is ready to buy if someone takes the time to explain things to him, to address him as an individual, to make it easy to buy, and if he is not dropped like a hot potato as soon as the act of purchase is concluded.

Faced with this state of play, the communication sector – since we must always put a name to things even before their existence is truly established – declared itself to be 'interactive'.

Technology came to the rescue, offering the means of communication to render the world of slogans and advertisements accessible to the general public; freefone helplines and customer charge cards for individual stores began to invade the market, beckoning to any wandering customer.

The pleasure of purchasing must go hand in hand with the pleasure of selling. Buyers and sellers depend on one another for their mutual existence and neither one should enjoy a dominant position over the other. If you know how to buy then you automatically know how to sell, as the procedure is exactly the same. Bernard Tapie, flamboyant French businessman and owner of Olympic Marseille football club, when I asked him how he bought a business, replied 'I never bought up any business, I sold myself to the management as the best company rescuer!'

Today it seems to be an established fact, you have to sell: but faced with the current transformation in the art of selling, how do you acquire the frame of mind necessary to do so? How, when and why should we transform ourselves into a salesperson? Old habits die hard and our automatic reactions tell us to dissociate our daily conduct from that of a seller; your position as a seller could be equated with the result of putting on a uniform, suddenly you endorse an entire attitude. Yet the bottom line is, and this is precisely the message of this book, that 'everything sells'. A smile can sell, an attitude, the coffee you bring, the magazine you offer, the flower arrangement in the office, everything can sell right down to the colour of your walls. Everything sells but also 'everyone is a seller' and especially those who think they don't have to be: hard working administrators or grumpy managing directors, everyone making an appearance in professional life is selling.

The aim of this book is to focus on these areas within selling, which permit the total sale: not only that of the product or service but also of the brand image. Each time we purchase a product we buy an image and the desire for that image is very often subconsciously as strong as the desire for the product: 'My perfume is Chanel', 'I read the time in Cartier' and 'I'm an active woman if I wear...'

How, therefore, can a brand name preserve its territory and power if those who directly or indirectly represent it don't feel themselves to be in any way responsible?

What a shame that the term 'representative' should be so completely discredited, directly associated with 'smooth talker' – the vacuum cleaner salesman who leans persistently on your doorbell. We've forsaken its usage and paraphrased it with terms which are supposed to be more respectable and acceptable.

We are all 'representatives', whether of the company we work for, the brand name we're promoting or even of our country of origin.

Selling cannot really come into its own without a sense of pride in belonging, you can't sell yourself well unless you are level-headed and self confident.

Our aim therefore is to attempt to list all the selling signposts, apparent or otherwise, which surround us in our professional lives.

Every one of us is more frequently confronted by selling in all its guises. We shall attempt to rediscover this commercial sensitivity and examine ways of releasing the potential sales-person inside us all. This recognition will have a twofold effect of making sense of our professional lives and allowing each personality to express himself fully as an individual.

IMPROVING YOUR SELLING KNOW-HOW

Section 1
THE ART OF SELLING EXPLAINED

The present decade promises to be a period of great upheaval. All sectors are affected by the winds of change shaking the deepest foundations.

Whether it concerns political and economic world order resulting from the fall of communism, and a greater blending of left and right ideologies, or the graduates' abandoning of a career strategy in favour of self-development, the change is there. The common denominator of the multiple manifestations of change that are in progress is: the primary importance of the individual rather than the group. What has happened to 'the man in the street', 'the typical voter', or the so-called 'average housewife'? We are in the process of emerging from collective, mass systems right across the board whether they be political or economic.

The future lies in the recognition of the individual, the consumer. The full acknowledgement of the consumer – finally considered as an individual with a name, address and telephone number and not just a mere statistic – warns of a transformation in the sales world, which will take its slice of the action in this wave of fascination for 'personalization' by calling on its full range of talents. And what could be more personalised than the traditional meeting of that duo: Buyer and Seller?

Abandoned, even maligned during the era of advertising, selling is once again in the limelight, and must take account of this new situation. But let us first take a look at what has changed in the buyer's behaviour and, by implication, the art of selling.

9

NEW TRENDS IN PURCHASING
BEHAVIOUR

The desire to *have* has given way to the desire to *be*, a frame of mind well summed up by this formula which illustrates and embodies all that underlies the act of purchase.
'In the factory, we make cosmetics. In the store we sell hope.'
Charles Revlon (Managing Director of Revlon Beauty Products).

RECOGNITION

The desire to be: a growing interest in the knowledge of oneself and others has resulted in the development of a number of techniques until now listed under the somewhat controversial heading of the Irrational. Astrology, Morphology, Tarot cards and Numerology are all beginning to feature in our daily lives and possibly in our professional environment. Beyond a certain fascination for this type of thing, it's worth trying to understand the passion for it. We could see in it, to some extent, a thoughtful rejection of all forms of superficiality. This desire to go beyond appearances is not merely a reaction to a culture based on consumerism and materialism. This cult of the acquisitive gave rise to an attitude of relentless pursuit, an acceleration which by degrees is producing a kind of uniform sameness. Before a consumer differentiated himself – and thus existed! – by buying a certain type of product. Today this means of differentiation is made more and more difficult:
– a large majority of products is now available to the great majority of consumers
– competition has erased the distinctions between the products themselves.
And so it's becoming less and less a matter of finding something different from all his other possessions that leads the customer out to buy – what he is looking for is recognition of his individuality. The article bought becomes almost a pretext, while the context of the purchase assumes a new importance: the chat he will have had with the sales assistant, the cashier's smile, the style and atmosphere of the sales premises which will have recognized him as an individual are the real deciding factors for the consumer.

KNOW WHAT TO SAY

A few lines to banish from your repertoire:
- ☞ What are you looking for?
- ☞ Do you have something in mind?

These openings for gaining the customer's confidence are infinitely more effective:
- ☞ It's not that easy to make a choice with such a wide range of models on offer. Would you like me to sum up in a few words the merits of each one?
- ☞ Is there a particular aspect you've already decided on (brand, size, price...)? In that case let me just show you a few models.
- ☞ I get the strong impression that this is the one you're interested in. What's making you hesitate over it?

  'Talk to me about myself, it's the only thing that interests me.'
- ☞ With your complexion, Madam, an orange tone would suit you perfectly...
- ☞ Does your timetable allow you to examine your bank statements on a weekly basis or would you prefer a monthly statement?

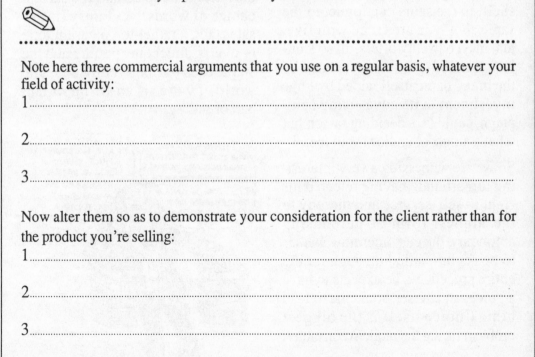

Note here three commercial arguments that you use on a regular basis, whatever your field of activity:

1 ....

2 ....

3 ....

Now alter them so as to demonstrate your consideration for the client rather than for the product you're selling:

1 ....

2 ....

3 ....

REASSURANCE

'In need of a little extra advice': this could be the the new consumer's motto.

The customer is no longer satisfied with the product on offer. The multitude of products, the profusion of brands, the constant urgings to buy leave him dizzy and fed up.

Saturation point has already been reached and his need lies elsewhere: *'Help me, I don't know which way to turn!'* The commercial proposition as such has lost its power to appeal. What can you do when on the same shelf, in the same catalogue, in the same shop you are faced with five, ten, maybe twenty offers, all so similar? Certainly, the dream created by the brand name itself, aided by huge investment in its advertising campaign, could be a deciding factor, but what a jungle of choice is out there!

So we are witnessing a very interesting turnaround: having rejected his right to self-service and thereby to the highest form of purchasing autonomy, the customer now wishes to be accompanied throughout the entire procedure: he expects to have a guide, an adviser, someone to lead him. Choice itself is the biggest problem facing the modern consumer:

'Choice, this limited freedom . . .' is the reason for his search for reassurance, his expectation that someone can simplify in an objective manner, his confusion with the market. And yet the customer would much prefer not to risk calling on the sales assistant for fear of being trapped by him, so it is up to the salesperson to make contact and open up the possibility for easy and comfortable discussion. He should opt for the role of ally when approaching a hesitant client and not adopt a conquering attitude which will arouse suspicion. A delicate situation which is controlled by the attitude adopted and the careful choice of words. A clumsy line of sales talk, a rather too pleasant tone or overly direct questioning and the spark dies out between you. The world of words is an all-important part of selling.

I HAVE READ ALL THE MOST INNOVATIVE MAGAZINES AND JOURNALS IN THE INDUSTRY SINCE 1975 ...THE JOURNAL OF CULINARY ART, COOKING TODAY etc

AND I HAVE NO DOUBT THAT THE GARLIC PRESS PRODUCED BY MOULINET IS BY FAR THE BEST

TIMESAVING

SOME TIMESAVING SERVICES WHICH ARE APPRECIATED BY CUSTOMERS:

– an answering machine with a pre-recorded message giving details of opening hours of the premises
– a preview of promotional campaigns
– a consumer hotline to give a quick response to all kinds of questions (stocks, colours, prices...)
– a service which takes orders by phone or fax
– a home delivery service
– directions on how to get to the premises
– brochures clearly outlining procedures for delivery and payment, instructions for use of apparatus
– a phone-in helpline to assist in the operation and maintenance of certain products
– clear indication of parking facilities convenient to the premises
– an evening or half-day specially reserved for loyal regular customers during busy periods (Christmas, January sales...)
– etc.

PERSONAL NOTES

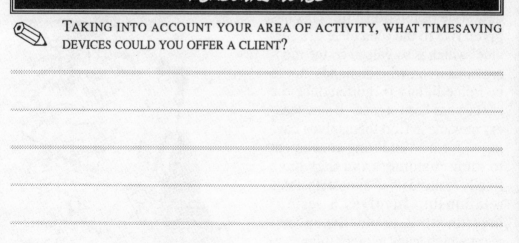

TAKING INTO ACCOUNT YOUR AREA OF ACTIVITY, WHAT TIMESAVING DEVICES COULD YOU OFFER A CLIENT?

WOOED AND MADE FAITHFUL

More than ever the customer now wants someone to take care of his needs but a surfeit of offers has made him more demanding. He is well aware that he is in the enviable position of 'consumer'. Pretentious lines of argument promoting the dream, once-in-a-lifetime article only make him smile. Thus the customer's demand associated with buying concerns not only the product itself but extends to the area of after-sales.

After-sales now consists of much more than the headings 'Claims' or 'Repairs' (with which it has long been associated). It's more a question of extending the honeymoon period following a purchase with a new style of relationship. This has given rise to the idea of 'extra service' which is so valued by the modern consumer, who demands not to be immediately forgotten once the cheque has been signed. Brand leaders nowadays find themselves having to form an enduring attachment to their customers and they have finally realised (well almost) that this relationship involves a serious investment. A productive investment which leads to other things: to new contacts, information, data...

Why?

– because the consumer is flattered by the individual attention he receives and is in fact 'hooked';

– because his future consumer choices are simplified by the personally targeted offers made to him;

– because his precious time is respected (he's saved needless journeys, he is advised throughout the buying process...).

And here is the final characteristic of the 'new' consumer: he is more concerned with 'value for time' than 'value for money'. The most important thing for him is to have the frame of mind necessary and enough free time to spend on his own personal pursuits! Thus the case for saving time is always an effective argument.

NEW TRENDS IN BUYING BEHAVIOUR: RECAP

OUT	IN
☞ Addressing groups or the masses	☞ The individual
☞ The desire to possess	☞ The need 'to be'
• large quantities of ordinary objects	• seeing through the decoys in the buying process
• rating the individual according to the goods he possesses (the 'nouveau riche' of the 60s)	• a self-centred satisfaction – service – hidden extras
• the show off	☞ The need to accompany the customer throughout the entire buying process
☞ The total autonomy of 'self- service' buying	☞ Expectation of a more lasting relationship with the brand name used
☞ The one-off sale	• The desire for something 'Extra'
☞ The single 'must have' product	☞ Personalized information
☞ The great advertising push	☞ Loyalty to the brand and its message
☞ Discount prices	☞ Value for money

FROM THE SPIRIT OF CONQUEST TO THE CULTURE OF MAINTAINING CUSTOMER LOYALTY

The customer has emerged from the 'silent target' syndrome whereby the sales approach was simply to force the greatest number possible to yield to persuasion. Today, a customer is won over individually and more slowly; step by step and never let go. The image of the aggressive salesman who must sell at all costs ('If I can't get past the door, I try the window') has become blurred to the advantage of the more intellectual salesman who prefers to build up and safeguard a steady, committed clientele over the years, disregarding the short-term gain.

This culture of maintaining customer loyalty fulfils the current expectations of consumers as well as the business's demands for profitability. Winning over a new customer costs four or five times more than the relations of a loyal and regular one.

The financial value of a loyal customer can be calculated using a formula borrowed from mail order/long-distance selling: namely, lifetime value. You arrive at this figure by multiplying the profit margins on each sale by the number of purchases you assume the customer will make in a given period of time, X, which corresponds to the average length of the commercial operation; the result establishes an index which allows you to gauge the contribution of each customer to the profits of the company.

Let's take for example, membership subscriptions to a national organization, which sends out a quarterly bulletin. To increase their membership, the organization offers increasingly attractive free gifts for the introduction of new subscribers. The aim of all this is to gain such a wide membership that leading brand names will agree to buy advertising space in its publication. It reaches the point, however, where the cost of gaining a reader is no longer profitable: an artificial and unhealthy situation especially that there is a national decrease in the purchase of advertising space. But it's here that we return to the consumer who tires of the pages and pages of ads in their favourite magazine. The worst consequence of this is the total lack of loyalty to the organization which results.

The bond which used to ensure the survival of the association or publication has disappeared. End of story!

DO YOU POSSESS SELLING POTENTIAL?

1. What would be (the most and the least) likely to encourage a customer to enter a sales premises?

A. a sales assistant engrossed in a telephone conversation	+	-
B. a sales assistant deep in discussion with another customer	+	-
C. an assistant who looks you straight in the eye	+	-
D. an assistant who makes a gesture of invitation to enter	+	-
E. an assistant who smiles at you	+	-

2. Once the customer is inside, what is your attitude?

A. you offer immediate assistance ....
B. a welcoming question ....
C. constant presence ....
D. a friendly indifference ....
E. you offer help only if you're asked for it ....

3. Arrange the following attitudes in ascending order of preference

IF THE CLIENT STOPS BEFORE A PARTICULAR ITEM, SHOULD THE SALEPERSON:

A. question his reason for stopping and his presumed choice ....
B. attract his attention to another product in the same line ....
C. steer his attention away from the product if it doesn't correspond to what
he's looking for ....
D. wait in silence for the customer to express his opinion ....

4. It's too expensive! What's your reaction?

A. it's a very fine article, sir, and not at all expensive ....
B. have you seen our competitors' prices? ....
C. too pricey in relation to what? ....
D. too expensive in itself, or too expensive for your pocket? ....

5. What, in your opinion, is the most commercial response to the situation where the client can't make up his mind between two items?

A. you know, it's not in my own interests to recommend one product over another ....
B. personally, I'd go for this one ....
C. it's up to you to consider what you need ....
D. let's both examine the use you'll be making of it ....

6. 'I'm going to think about it.' How do you reply to the customer?

A. don't spend too long thinking about it, you'll never be able to take advantage
of such an offer again ....
B. that's it, come back whenever you like ....
C. are you going to think it over to compare it with a similar article or because
you think it's not quite right for you? ....
D. you want to get your (husband's, colleague's) opinion? ....

17

CALCULATE YOUR SCORE

	NUMBER OF POINTS		NUMBER OF POINTS		NUMBER OF POINTS
1.		**2.**		**3.**	
A + 2	A - 3	A	3	A	4
B + 3	B - 2	B	5	B	1
C + 1	C - 4	C	1	C	2
D + 4	D - 1	D	2	D	3
E + 2	E - 1	E	4		
4.		**5.**		**6.**	
A	1	A	1	A	2
B	2	B	2	B	1
C	4	C	3	C	4
D	3	D	4	D	3

Over 25 points

You are already well aware of the subtlety involved in your relationship with the consumer. You belong to the new generation of sales personnel. Continue to exercise your listening skills to remain in step with the needs of your clientele.

15 – 25 points

You're almost there! Remember, the aim of the seller/buyer relationship is not to achieve a sale no matter what, it's more of a long-term alliance, based both on the power to seduce and the existence of a mutual faith. You can experience and experiment with this new mode of selling throughout this book. You will considerably enhance your existing selling instincts and thereby develop this part of your personality.

Less than 15 points

Your idea of the world of selling is slightly limited at the moment. You still feel that selling is an ignoble profession where the salesperson compromises his opinions to elicit agreement from his client. This book will give you a new perception of selling: it's all around you in your daily life and a mastery of selling skills will improve the quality of all your interpersonal relationships.

KEY TO ANALYSIS

1. A. Even if a client would prefer to be left to his own devices, a salesperson giving the impression of being mentally absent from the scene for whatever reasons would be regarded as a disincentive to buy.
   B. On the other hand, demonstrating an interest in another client acts as an incentive. He is even more reassured if others share his interest in a particular product.
   C. Instead of falling immediately under the charm of a salesperson, the client's initial reaction is to make good his escape. This slightly pushy invitation is actually seen as the trap, from which he would be incapable of extricating himself once caught. It's not easy to find the correct balance somewhere between welcome availability and total absence!
   D. This perhaps is used as a gesture to welcome the customer who has decided to come into the sales premises. Until then, such a gesture might seem too forthcoming and make the customer perversely back off.
   E. A smile is in effect the welcoming sign which bridges this gap and embodies both the idea of desirable availability and a reassuring discretion on the part of the salesperson. It's the best way to inspire confidence in the client: it means that his presence on the premises is acknowledged but he won't be harassed.

2. A. The immediate offer of assistance is a double-edged sword. Effective and extremely well received if the customer has decided on his choice or is in a hurry, it can really kill off his enthusiasm if he is 'just looking', or simply wants to dream a little.
   B. A welcoming question reinforces the salesperson's smile. In any case, let the customer decide whether or not he wishes to seek immediate assistance.
   C. The assistant should measure his level of exposure carefully for fear of being perceived as a hovering presence rather than simply being ready to help. Otherwise he could run the risk of distracting the client from the business of choosing what to buy as he feels he has to resist the pressure of constant attendance.
   D. A friendly indifference could never really be regarded as the most enlightened sales technique; it leaves the potential buyer entirely on his own. The salesperson loses his identity as guide and adviser and merely melts into the background, becoming another feature of the shop display, and someone you wouldn't be bothered looking to for information.
   E. Waiting for a question to open up communication lines is a more acceptable attitude so long as the customer ultimately does ask one! An air of indifference can be disconcerting for the customer; it should be absolutely clear from the outset that the salesperson is at his complete disposal.

3. A. In the case of a prospective client lingering over a particular product, the salesperson should recognize an opportunity to point out its different features. The art of the salesperson in this instance lies in detecting an interested silence and in anticipating unexpressed queries.
   B. Often caused by an over-zealous attitude, deflecting the customer's attention is not the most productive attitude.
   C. This approach resembles the previous one but includes another element. If we accept that the client is king, we accept that he can broaden his choice when he sees the articles on offer on the premises. Therefore, if his initial demand lies in another direction the salesperson should not emphasize the 'versatility' of the customer.
   D. If listening is a supremely desirable quality in the area of sales then passivity is not. If the customer is given the opportunity to air his arguments and enthusiasm for a product the salesperson can take them up and deal with each one in turn to be more convincing.

Our reader reacted like a feckless girl who pockets the presents and then goes somewhere else.

The great problem of our time is that we have pushed the entire range of the tricks and devices of the hard, fast sell and have ultimately disappointed the consumer.

DEVELOPMENT OF THE STAGES IN SELLING

Compared with the classic sales procedures we have made some progress over the last two decades in enhancing and multiplying the strategies used in selling.

From a threefold strategy:

1) Contact (en masse)
2) Persuade (without concession)
3) Sell (and afterwards?)

It has developed into a fourfold one:

1) Target (you now have a better idea of whom you're addressing)
2) Contact
3) Persuade
4) Sell

To arrive at today's fivefold strategy, the aim of the fifth point being the creation of a long-lasting relationship:

1) Target/Personalize
2) Contact

3) Listen in order to persuade
4) To 'make' them buy
5) Construct a profitable relationship with the client.

So, in order to achieve this result, commercial language must rid itself of several bad habits:

– Blaming the client

Making the client feel he is at fault is a widely employed technique and one which makes a relationship based on trust impossible:

NOT SO EASILY FOOLED:

– the customer is better educated these days and so can often see through the repertoire and technique of the salesperson. He won't be so easy to convince as he used to be.

SCEPTICAL:

– what to expect from a brand name or a salesperson who sets out to put you, the customer, in the wrong?

FOR EXAMPLE:

Customer: 'I would prefer to buy a pure wool jumper rather than a synthetic one.'

Response of a 70s Salesperson: 'Of course it's true that up to now wool was the warmest material but now these new fibres are far superior!' The underlying implication is that you are a year out of date and you're not really well informed.

KEY TO ANALYSIS

4. A. This inflexible and outraged attitude may well demonstrate an unshakeable faith in your products, but what a lack of sensitivity towards your customer.
   Not only will this product remain on the shelf, but you can be sure that your shop will never see hide nor hair of this particular client in the near future. To accuse a customer of being both stingy 'not at all expensive' and lacking in any sense of taste 'it's a very fine article', is not a very subtle move.
   B. This attitude is an attempt to put a degree of blame on to the customer who is by implication being reproached for shopping haphazardly, without getting any information on current price rates. Two outcomes are possible here: either the customer has in fact studied the going rate and replies 'You're quite right I have, and they're a damn sight more attractive than yours, so I'm off back there!', or in the same vein: 'What a good idea, I will check out the competition!' An attitude which gets results...for the competition!
   C. It's a much better strategy to accord the customer his right to express a negative attitude about the product without calling into question his solvency or his level of education!
   D. To help the customer reply by suggesting an alternative usually works quite well. But be careful, we're talking about money here, a sensitive if not taboo topic, so one might expect a reply like 'too expensive in itself'. Furthermore the argument that the price of the article has been fairly calculated tends to show that it is the second option which concerns the customer, 'too expensive for your pocket'. Who wants to hear that?

5. A. As the customer doesn't care about the salesperson's interests, this attitude of 'offloading' the responsibility leaves the client feeling abandoned at the most crucial point of the sale, the final choice and tying up of the deal. The client is thus left completely to his own devices just at the moment when his need for reassurance is greatest.
   B. Likewise the personal tastes of the salesperson are of no help whatsoever unless the customer expressly asks for this kind of advice. The salesperson is distancing himself from his goal: the tracking down of his client's expectations. More in touch with his own needs than those of his customer he will not be there when the customer needs him most – at the point of making his decision.
   C. Spot on! This salesperson has understood everything, but he is still neglecting his role as companion to the buyer in the process of making a purchase. The moment of choosing is a crucial one and the salesperson needs to focus his energies on this aspect of the sale.
   D. Excellent! Here is the perfect combination of guide and adviser that is expected. A model argument is based on the information given by the customer, and the steps of reassurance and confidence building are completed naturally without forcing the issue.

6. A. This pretext of the 'limited offer' is too unsubtle to be effective. It is too often a transparent sales device and thus provokes suspicion.
   B. This shows a lack of drive on the salesperson's part. Does he really want to sell?
   C. This sales technique, unlike the previous one, demonstrates the seller's interest in his client. Impressed by this show of attention, he will take into account both the quality of the product on offer and the quality of the sales consultation when reaching a decision.
   D. Anticipating this reaction is none the less risky for winding up the deal. The salesperson is actively helping the client to make his escape by ascribing his motives of indecision to a sphere outside the immediate territory of the sale. The client has been helpfully supplied with an excuse for his uncertainty and naturally enough he defers making the decision to buy!

Response of a 90s Salesperson: 'Do you mean you prefer wool for its ability to keep its shape or for its warmth?'

☞ Consideration for the customer's point of view and a conversation opener.

The technical spiel, often unintelligible for the customer...

A common occurrence in certain sectors (car industry, information technology, banking...) this type of discussion doesn't really make for dialogue as the customer is rather left out of things. The overuse of technical jargon usually arises from a need for the salesperson himself to feel secure and confident.

FOR EXAMPLE:

A 70s Salesperson : 'And it also has a front to back engine with double overhead camshaft!'
Customer: 'Oh yes?'

A 90s Salesperson: 'It has been fitted with a new type of engine which increases its power and responsiveness.'

This type of complex technical demonstration must give way to simplicity, and so, too, sensationalizing hype must be replaced by explanation.

A line of argument which has no basis in the expressed requirements of the customer

FOR EXAMPLE:

70s Salesperson: 'I'm sure you will agree that what counts today is the operating speed of these products, so I have an excellent fax machine to show you...'
Customer: 'Yes but...'
90s Salesperson: 'Are you more concerned with the operating speed of the fax machine you're looking for, or would you prefer it to be easy to use?'

IMPROVE YOUR LISTENING POWERS

☞ Be alert not only to the expressed needs of your customer but also to those unstated.

☞ Allocate at least half the negotiation time to listening.

☞ Don't give your opinion until the customer has been allowed to express theirs in full.

☞ Remain attentive even if your customer is longwinded and digressive.

☞ Never interrupt the customer.

☞ Do not jump to conclusions by anticipating your prospective client's expectations, you might miss out on an important aspect of the negotiation.

☞ Do ask questions (at least one) even if you don't feel it's necessary: it's proof of your attention and interest.

☞ Do not try to anticipate what your customer is going to say: 'Stop right there, I know exactly what you're looking for...'

☞ Address yourself to more than one of a group you may be dealing with – the decision-maker may not always be the person doing the talking.

☞ Make a point of committing faces, voices and names to memory.

THE IMPORTANCE OF SERVICE

The well-known rule of the USP, the Unique Selling Point, introduced by Rosser Reeves, which involves promoting one sole advantage of a product only, has doubled up to include a second concept the 'Extra Value Proposition'. This means adding a 'Plus' to the product in the form of service. Thus the new generation salesperson can incorporate the following equation into his art:

$$QUALITY = PRODUCT + SERVICE$$

An equation which draws on his creative powers, the salesperson must try his hand at psychology, as it's no longer enough to learn a technique off by heart:
'What's going to please the client?'
This suggests the evolution of a new attitude for all those having a direct or indirect influence on sales. This attitude supposes they can act in a positive fashion in three types of relationship:

Relationship with the company
Pride in belonging
– Adherence to the objectives and ventures of the company
– Team spirit: colleague/colleague; section/section)

Relationship with oneself
Confidence in your own professional capabilities
– Self-confidence
– Awareness of personal strengths and weaknesses
– Feeling at ease in the post you hold

Relationships with others
(Clients, prospective clients, general public)
– Relaxed contact
– Open, friendly manner
– Listening
– Initiative
– Dealing with problems
– An ability to make people welcome

TRAVEL AGENTS 2000
EGYPTE —
AND AS AN EXTRA SERVICE, WE WATER YOUR PLANTS WHILE YOU'RE AWAY!

THREE RULES OF CONDUCT FOR A SUCCESSFUL SALES CONSULTATION

1 TAKE YOUR TIME
> Silence or the 'yes' which is not necessarily to be taken as a sign of agreement should not be interpreted as a signal for the rapid conclusion of a sale.

2 LOVE YOUR CLIENT AS MUCH AS YOUR PRODUCT
> Your line of argument should be adapted to the client's needs rather than the product you're selling.

3 LISTEN!
> Every proposition must tap into an expressed desire or plan on the part of the client.

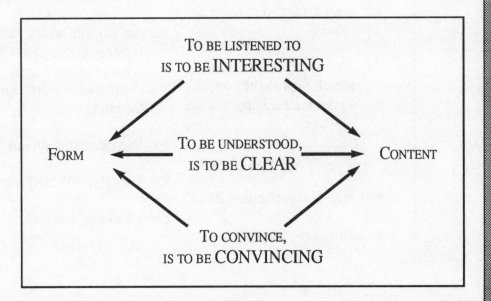

TO BE LISTENED TO IS TO BE **INTERESTING**

FORM — TO BE UNDERSTOOD, IS TO BE **CLEAR** — CONTENT

TO CONVINCE, IS TO BE **CONVINCING**

THE NEW SALES PROCESS: RECAP

OUT	IN
☞ The spirit of conquest based on short-term gain	☞ The culture of customer loyalty
☞ The fast-talking 'desperado' type salesperson	☞ The salesperson as 'adviser'
☞ The big push promotion to boost immediate sales figures	☞ 'Lifetime Value'
	☞ A genuine interest in and interaction with the client.
☞ Customer passivity	☞ Constant adaptation to suit the needs of the client
☞ Standardized sales techniques	
☞ The type of persuasion which reproaches or presumes the agreement of the customer	☞ An attitude which favours listening, simplicity and which taps into the expressed requirements of the client
☞ Esoteric technical jargon	☞ 'No more smooth talk'
☞ The 'Unique Selling Point'	☞ The 'Extra Value Point'
☞ Thinking 'product'	☞ Thinking 'service'

Section 2
NEW SALES TERRITORY

'WHAT ARE YOU SELLING?'

Companies are like a huge forest with a 'salesperson' behind every tree. In many firms they seem reluctant to reveal themselves and go to great lengths to avoid facilitating a sale. You've met them.

Described below are some examples of such breakdowns in commercial relations. At the end of each scenario, the correct attitude has been defined, but we particularly emphasize the situations on which so much depends even though the people concerned are not selling directly. They are presenting an image of the company, however, that will influence whether a sale takes place or not.

DISASTROUS SCENARIOS AND DISASTROUS RESPONSES

Scene: Reception

You have an appointment with Mr Murray, Head of Sales. You enter the reception area and head in the direction of the receptionist. The first contact with a company is sometimes disconcerting...

– *She doesn't raise her eyes from her crossword until you address her directly.*

– *She heaves a great sigh as she notices your approach and tries to appear extremely busy.*

– *She smiles in your direction but continues an evidently intense conversation with a colleague. After some minutes, on remembering your presence, she finally addresses you: 'Yes, sir?'*

– *She launches straight into conversation with you, telling you all about her mediocre working conditions.*

Mr Murray will be a little late... You are made aware of this in the following manner:

– *'I'm afraid you're out of luck, sir, but it's always like this with him!'*

  VISITOR: *'Tell me, has my arrival been announced?'*

  RECEPTIONIST: *'Yes, of course! The only reason I'm not calling you is because he's not in yet!'*
  'I hope he hasn't forgotten your appointment!'

Scene: Secretarial Service

A few days later you telephone Mr Murray. You would like some additional information on his products. The telephonist connects you with his secretary who will be either suspicious or just plain disagreeable: that's the norm...

You introduce yourself.

– *'Mr...? Does he know you?'*

– *'I really can't put you through, you see we are extremely busy today, could you call back tomorrow?'*

– *'I'll try to put you through but with this new phone system I'm not sure it'll work. If you are cut off do call back!'*

– *'But you only saw him yesterday, what is going on?'*

– *'I'll just see if I can disturb him.'*

The blocking or filtering of calls at secretarial level constitutes a serious problem. This over-protective attitude towards the executive brings about the following anomaly: 60 per cent of blocked calls result in the loss of a potential customer to the company. It's obvious that this system of filtering calls, used in so many companies, needs a complete overhaul:

– By taking the time to establish a clear line of instruction with the secretaries.

– By being more flexible about accepting a call.

The sales directors of large American companies admit to always taking calls from people they don't know: that's where the business comes from . . .

THE COLOUR OF THE RECEPTIONIST'S LIPSTICK

It's not enough to cater to his needs or wants. What is significant from the visitor's point of view is that he feels that he is expected, that consideration is shown if problems crop up (waiting, delays...) and that he receives considerate attention. It should be understood that a receptionist must always give the impression of being on the visitor's side rather than the company's, this being one of the few occasions when such a relationship is desirable.

Scene: Technical Services

The product which you have bought from Mr Murray required an installation team to assemble it on your premises. Brief encounter – lasting impression...

– *The team arrives two hours late, offers no excuse or explanation, and begins a noisy installation with complete disregard for the fact that your meeting is in progress in the neighbouring office.*

– *They've gone ... Now all you have to do is call in a firm of contract cleaners.*

– *They've left the offices on tiptoe. Their discretion is such that they have left no trace of ever having been there: not a single instruction for use or maintenance of your equipment...*

– *There's a piece missing – you will see them again if you can find them, which seems to be the difficulty despite the importance of such a service to any trading company...*

There are certain sections within a company which are given so little consideration that they become mere 'phantom' figures within the overall infrastructure. Don't they know that they too have an image to maintain? Have they been informed of the importance and consequences of the quality of their work? Apart from their technical performance, are they made aware of the professional conduct expected of them? They usually appear at the most sensitive stage, the implementation or 'carrying out' of the sale. They are the people responsible for this final 'relay' in the strategy of accompanying the client. To neglect this final stage means to take a risk. Disappointment after the conclusion of a sale is viewed by the customer as an act of unforgivable betrayal.

Being able to rely on a technical services department with a positive attitude is a real commercial asset for a business, as can be seen from the following case of a fuel delivery company:

This particular business, with no increase in sales for over two years, was desperately seeking some method of improving the figures. The sales director launched a survey of his target area, the residents of the London suburbs. The results yielded two phenomena:

– no notable change in the product itself was expected;

– the image attributed to a fuel delivery company was strongly linked to the behaviour of the actual deliverers .

The conclusion is obvious: they must be mobilized. The training department had to come up with a way to incorporate that 'extra' something so necessary to their service, and so devised a programme of 'life skill' for the driver-deliverers. They in turn learned through a series of precise instructions (to wipe your feet before entering the house, not to crush the flower beds with the fuel pipe, to sweep up after you've finished...) to 'please' the housewives. The commercial results more than made up for the effort involved.

Scene: Accounts Department

You are slightly behind with payment as a result of a temporary cash flow problem. Murray's accountant contacts you.
The shock is a rude one...
- *'Listen, I have already extended the agreed date of payment by ten days! We won't wait a day longer!'*
- *'It has come to our attention that there is a slight delay in your payment. You are evidently experiencing cash flow difficulties, if this is the case say so!'*
- *'I'm calling to inform you that your case is now in the hands of our lawyers, we do this systematically here.'*
- *'I knew your company had a bad reputation with suppliers. This*

merely confirms my suspicions!'
More than ever before, accounting now plays an essential commercial role. The utility companies are battling to collect arrears in reasonable instalment payments. What about you? Are you sufficiently aware that payment negotiations are an integral part of selling, right up to cashing the cheque? A successful sale can still leave a bad taste if a grumpy accountant refuses to listen.
As at all other stages of the commercial seduction, the customer should be allowed to do the talking. At this crucial stage more so than at any other, interaction does pay off. In this way all those accountants hidden behind their demand notices, their systematic debt recovery procedures and their administrative discourse will from now on be considered 'out'. This service will have to develop an ear and open up the communication lines for successful dialogue: a marked increase has been shown in successful debt recovery when telephone marketing techniques have been employed; the 'bad' payer really appreciates having an opportunity to explain his reasons for delaying payment (he is somewhat relieved by being allowed to explain), and he immediately becomes an active participant in the search for a solution to the financial problem.

AIDING AND ABETTING A SALE . . .

FUNCTION/JOB	NATURE OF INVOLVEMENT WITH SALES	DEGREE OF AWARENESS OF THIS INFLUENCE ON SALES (*strong, moderate, weak*)

... IN YOUR PROFESSIONAL ENVIRONMENT

NATURE OF DEFICIENCIES TO BE CORRECTED	DESIRABLE SOLUTIONS/ DEVELOPMENTS	WHERE TO DRAW THE LINE

Scene: Managing Director

You meet Mr Murray at a trade exhibition. He is accompanied by his managing director who is intoduced to you.

The encounter leaves you sceptical...

– *'Mr...? Ah, so we do business together?'*

– *Distracted greeting, looking elsewhere, sudden relief: 'Ah, I think I see Mr Bigbucks over there, I really must go over and say hello to him! See you soon.'*

– *'Delighted to meet you, Mr... So what do you think of our products? Isn't it true to say we're the best? I'm quite sure that Murray has given you all the assistance you need and don't hesitate to call me directly if needs be, okay?'*

The correct sales attitude for a director confronted with a client is to demonstrate support for his employees. The customer should feel reassured on two counts:

– of the competence of the person he usually deals with
– of the significance of his position as client no matter what size account he represents (little fish grow into big fish). Thus the conduct of a director should demonstrate how much he values both his sales representative and his client. The notion that everyone's a winner should underline his overall sales campaign.

Finally, the client should be able to tell from the director's attitude that the person he usually deals with holds a position of real power at the heart of the company.

This perception has a direct bearing on his sense of satisfaction in his position as client: the more important he feels the salesperson to be, the more likely he is to feel a valued customer.

ALL OF US ARE SALESPEOPLE?

Within a company we have found that selling touches on a number of areas that we certainly wouldn't have considered at the outset. Equally true is the fact that selling is closely linked with many more professions than we would have considered at first.

Politics

Always on the lookout for a voter's voice to join their own, elected representatives are, however, less than ready to listen, and this neglect on their part can have serious consequences. This one-sided communication has resulted in the all too familiar speech, the hackneyed phrase and the long-winded rhetoric of the politician.

The real problem facing politics today is this great absence of interaction. The winds of change blowing through political party HQs will no doubt herald a new approach based to a greater extent on the actual needs and expectations of the electorate rather than those of the candidates themselves. This state of affairs implies a need for a new political attitude rather more like that which is present in sales. It will be less a question of being elected or re-elected than of making themselves the chosen one.

There are some already enlightened among them who do incorporate more interactive strategies into their campaigns. They lend a satisfactory ear to their public and thus maximize personal contact. Take the case of the mayor of a constituency of X number of inhabitants who has introduced a new service for his constituents: 'Hello, Mr Mayor'. This freefone line allows any member of the public to question the mayor directly on any issue which is on his mind. The answer is given either on the spot by the councillor manning the service or in the following edition of the local council news. It must be added of course that the Mayor himself takes calls personally two hours a week, on Saturday!

The large so-called 'public service' industries

These industries distributing water, gas and electricity do not subscribe to the law of supply and demand. Their services by their very nature are in demand. However, selling is an important consideration here but is seen in a different light. These companies have observed a gradual alienation creeping in as a result of their near monopolistic position in society. This special status has created a divide between them and their consumer public and led to a developing scepticism about the quality of their services. So it became incumbent upon them to 'sell' a new image of themselves as caring companies sharing the concerns of their consumers, giving them a say in matters and a certain part to play in the management of crisis situations. The Water Board knew exactly how to play the game, placing at the public's disposition 'Information Drinking Water'. This freefone number gives everyone access to information concerning the degree of safety of the drinking water in their area. This free service is also aimed at answering questions born out of fear of 'risky' water supplies: 'Is it all right to give the tap-water to my baby?'

The immediate benefit of this operation is twofold:
- to demonstrate how a very large company can be both close to and at the service of its consumers
- to diminish the harmful effects of rumour by being completely frank and open with its information.

Administration

The first sign of a shift in thinking towards a sales mentality is usually a modification of administrative terminology to embrace a more commercial vocabulary. The terms 'subscriber' or 'user' are being gradually abandoned in favour of that long-forgotten term 'customer'.

The birth of a culture centred on customer satisfaction is causing great disturbance to the structures of large organizations and to people in general. British Telecom and the Post Office are the first to set the wheels in motion. Apart from launching new services intended to meet the needs of their newly identifiable consumer 'targets', the emphasis is soundly placed on the importance of training personnel. Just as the 'user' has turned into a 'customer' so the civil servant has become a 'salesperson', selling a product, an image of his company and no longer of its administration, and finally, he is selling himself. For in this sector, the hitherto undesirable image of the civil servant will be the biggest obstacle in the path of the advent of the spirit of selling. It takes a lot of imagination to deal with the notion of someone responsible for customer relations taking the place of the scowling or indifferent counter clerk we have put up with for so long. This is the area that selling has to target and move into: a new demeanour (and therefore a new image) for these 'ex-civil servants'. The quality of their contact with the public will be the most telling ingredient in this recipe for change.

SELLING IS EVERYWHERE

Here it is, selling is everywhere! Even the most resistant sectors are gradually tuning into the idea. Giving an ear to the customer no matter who he is, and adapting the offer to suit his requirements on a long-term basis sums up this new spirit of universal selling. So take a look around you, you will see the elements of selling behaviour in the most unexpected places.

☞ *You are at the hairdresser's, ask yourself: what is the stylist selling?*
    – a feeling of well-being
    – suggestions on products suitable for your hair type
    – advice and tips

CUSTOMER LOYALTY TO THE SALON

☞ *You are staying at a winter sports resort, what are the instructors selling?*
    – *joie de vivre* (smiling and tanned)
    – a feeling of security

IMAGE OF THE RESORT

☞ *You're in a restaurant, what is the waitress selling?*
    – the feeling of being made welcome, recognized
    – a feeling of well-being (thoughtfulness, warmth)
    – a whetting of the appetite (description of the dishes on offer)

FIDELITY TO THE RESTAURANT

☞ *You are paying for your goods at the supermarket checkout, what is the cashier selling?*
    – speed and efficiency
    – friendly contact (more strongly felt, because it is the only source of human contact in a large supermarket)

THE INDIVIDUALITY OF THE SHOP

And the examples are endless! Selling is present in all functions which involve contact no matter what the nature of that contact is. Nor is this limited to those with a consumer public. It also applies to journalists, financiers, authorities, suppliers and even your own colleagues.

WHAT ARE YOU SELLING?

Who are you dealing with?

☞ Customers/Prospects: ....

☞ Other: ....

What are you selling them?

☞ A definite service: ....

☞ Certain professional conduct: ....

On what particular occasion(s) do you employ your sales behaviour?

....

What do you think are the strengths of your sales behaviour?

....

And what points could you improve upon?

....

Who else could suffer as a result of these deficiencies?

....

Would you like to be better informed of the consequences of your attitude?

☞ In what way? ....

☞ By whom? ....

☞ With a view to what? ....

Section 2
INVISIBLE SELLING

If each of us is a salesperson then we are also going to see that *Everything Sells*. A sale is born of the coming together of many elements and its success depends largely on human behaviour. Each of us is involved no matter what his role and much also depends on how attractive the sales premises are. By this we mean the background elements which impose themselves on the potential client's judgement. These can be grouped into five categories:

1. The ergonomics of the premises
2. The appearance and behaviour of the employees
3. The overall general organization
4. The company correspondence
5. The ability to adapt to fashion trends or tendencies

These elements are essentially 'passive' in the area of sales as they are associated more with the company culture than its commercial strategy. However, they do have a profound influence on the customer's decision-making. Why? Because the commercial proposition appeals to the entirety of the customer's brain: both the left side (reason) and the right side (emotion). Thus, for a salesperson to focus only on the rational aspects of the sale is to deprive himself of 50 per cent of clinching arguments!

The client's impression of the service on offer will be formed for the most part by subjective considerations. These can be infinitely variable and essentially difficult to control. They could range from the perceived advantages of the product to the colour of the salesman's tie and include the originality of the music recorded on the holding line of the telephone system. Also, it is important to bear in mind that a customer is apt to perceive things other than what is being shown to him and this is a key factor in the success of the sale.

Ignoring the sales ambience no longer pays off. It's a far better strategy to sit up and look at the full extent to which your personal capabilities and the company as a whole can maximize input in the area of 'invisible' selling. Put yourself in the shoes of a potential customer for a few moments and reply to the questions that arise, using his eyes, nose, ears and his subjectivity. This procedure will be, in effect, a kind of examination of conscience and must be repeated for each of the aforementioned five categories. On each occasion we will also supply our own perspective of the issue.

THE IMPORTANCE OF THE PREMISES

The look of the premises is the first detail considered in the commercial process and far too many businesses don't pay enough attention to this 'first impression', and remember, you never get a second chance to make a first impression. Giving your premises a plus ranking in the selling stakes doesn't necessarily involve formulating an extravagant strategic concept, it just means being led by common sense and imagining what you would like to see if you were the customer. The commercial attractiveness of the premises is perceived at three levels.

1– The 'necessary minimum'

This refers to the existence of the basic facilities necessary to give visitors the impression of a smooth running and professional organization. It's not a question here of adding little extras but of eliminating any noticeable defects. This first level includes in particular:

☞ CLEAR INTERIOR AND EXTERIOR SIGNS: the intended visitor's 'route' should be easily recognizable. The company site itself, the reception area, parking facilities, toilets, lifts, etc should all be clearly marked.

☞ A WAITING AREA which is clean and quiet
  - Well co-ordinated furniture and decoration in good repair.
  - An area sufficiently removed from the daily routine of company business (the customer should not be a witness to any conversations or incidents). Even if you attach no great importance to them, they may induce a hostile or suspicious reaction on the part of your customer.

ARE YOU CAPITALIZING ON EVERY ASPECT OF SELLING?

When a visitor enters your premises, what's the first thing he notices?
- ☞ The colour of the rug? ....
- ☞ The stacked up boxes which should have been placed in the storage area two days ago? ....
- ☞ The portrait of your company director? ....
- ☞ Other (specify)

Your visitor is waiting at reception. What can he hear?
- ☞ Laughter from the neighbouring office? ....
- ☞ The telephone operator's personal calls? ....
- ☞ Murray shouting at his secretary? ....
- ☞ Other (specify)

What does he see?
- ☞ The plant on the point of giving up the ghost? ....
- ☞ The receptionist's knees? ....
- ☞ Last week's *Independent*? ....
- ☞ Other (specify)

He is directed to your office, what does he notice in the corridors?
- ☞ That the warmth of reception is missing from the rest of the premises? ....
- ☞ The coffee machine surrounded by its caffeine addicts? ....
- ☞ Total silence: the offices are closed, where are the employees? ....
- ☞ Other (specify)

He enters your office, what's the first thing he notices?
- ☞ The old-fashioned and ill-matching office furniture? ....
- ☞ The cold coffee and wilting sandwich sitting on a desk? ....
- ☞ The smell of cigarette smoke? ....
- ☞ Other (specify)

– A few specialist magazines relevant to your field of business. It is preferable to hand over your own company brochures directly with any necessary comments on their content.

– A floral arrangement (provided this does not consist of a plastic plant or greenery in an advanced state of decay).

– 'Non-aggressive' decor in keeping with the serious image of the company. Whether the feeling of aggression is provoked by a heavy-handed style of decoration or a total lack of aesthetic effort, it is negative in effect. The customer shouldn't really be aware of the decor. He should, on the other hand, notice your company logo, the warm welcome at reception, and the atmosphere that you would like to communicate to him. The decor in itself is only there to complement these aspects, it should not become the essential. Be wary of originality at all costs: all manner of tastes being possible, your choice risks being in real danger of not appealing to the majority of customers. A lack of basic concern for the aesthetics of the surroundings is equally unwise because it is frequently perceived as the result of a neglectful and careless attitude.

2 – 'Enhancing the value of commercial salestalk'

You should consider using your commercial premises to promote the company message. This chiefly implies the reinforcement of this message through the image of the company, by attention to details such as the holding time on the phone lines or time spent waiting by the customer in the reception areas...

☞ PRE-RECORDED TELEPHONE MESSAGE

At present, if you are lucky enough to escape Vivaldi's *Four Seasons*, you will probably find yourself listening to a recorded message. Usually the average holding time on the line is between one and a half and two minutes. This gives you plenty of time to talk to your customers! Record up-to-date messages, adapting them to the seasons or the launch of new products.

☞ MAKE AVAILABLE TO THE CUSTOMER A BOOK OF PRESS CUTTINGS concerning your company. Press reports which are concise in their description of your products or services will be more convincing to the customer than long speeches. Reassured by your credibility, he will be more receptive to your sales pitch.

BETTER SIGNS FOR BETTER SELLING

25 per cent of the customer's time on the sales premises is spent in the search for information: time wasted, which develops a feeling of aggression directed at the possible guilty party: the salesperson.

SOME BASIC TIPS

☞ Don't go over the top on the creative aspect of the signposting, nobody expects Picasso.

☞ Do not be discreet (for once). You can never have too many signs.

☞ Use COLOUR.

☞ Have you considered placing signs on the ground?

☞ Classification should be distinct (possibly with sub-titles in a second language).

☞ Labels should be clear and readable.

☞ Avoid the use of abbreviations.

☞ Do not mix up the general documentation with instructions for use.

☞ Insist on uniforms so that customers can find the salespeople.

☞ Why not supply badges with their names on them?

☞ Highlight the information counters (which do supply information!).

☞ Designate well indicated consultation zones.

☞ Let's hail a return to the good old days, the nostalgia of the service and reception: porters, delivery, canopies over the entrance, uniforms with braid trimming...

☞ DISPLAY RECENT ACCOMPLISHMENTS, from the current advertising campaign or work published by the company. All the time this process should remain low-key. The client should never feel that he has been trapped by an egocentric company, a subtle balance should be observed between the attention you want to receive from the client and the attention you pay him.

3 – The commercial 'plus'

Some companies, always on the lookout for ways to differ from the competition, highlight any advantages on their premises which could constitute a plus in the eyes of their customers. Besides a particularly well-appointed reception, personalized message of welcome, offers of coffee or other refreshments, availability of cloakroom facilities – real 'services' are offered to the client/visitor: trolleys, telephone facilities, cafés and restaurant areas, (some of the more plush London restaurants are situated on business premises!), supervised play areas for children (at IKEA, for example)...the sales premises develops a strong and active role in the entire commercial process by attracting customers,

more or less subconsciously, to come back again: because it's EASIER, because it's more PLEASANT, and because the attention given to small details which affect the customer is a sign of the highest quality service.

APPEARANCE AND BEHAVIOUR

'Even when naked, we remain clothed by our behaviour.' (ROLAND BARTHES)

...And when dressed we are clothed by our appearance! The clothing worn and the paraphernalia (accessories, jewellery, make-up) require the same level of consideration for others as do hygiene and cleanliness. It's not necessary to go back over the need to care for our appearance in a general sense, but we are going to examine this aspect since it may back us up when making a sale.

The outfit you are wearing and the impression it makes on your customer, is the first message he will receive from you. It shouldn't be turned into an announcement. Three simple rules will help to stack the cards in your favour.

HYGIENE!
EXAMINATION OF CONSCIENCE

Do you ventilate your office/sales premises?
- ☞ Several times a day ....
- ☞ Less often ....
- ☞ I use a deodorising spray to get rid of the smell of tobacco ....

Your deodorant, does it last all day long?
- ☞ Yes, no problem ....
- ☞ I have to re-apply it several times a day ....
- ☞ I don't know ....

During lunch, do you think of the effect of certain ingredients on your breath? (spices, alcohol, garlic)?
- ☞ Yes, always ....
- ☞ No, I never consider it ....
- ☞ From now on I'll leave these things until the evening or the weekend ....

You get a stain on your tie just before an important appointment, what do you do?
- ☞ You change or run out and buy another ....
- ☞ You employ every means to try to clean it off, then give up when it starts to develop a ring round it ....
- ☞ It doesn't matter, anyway it doesn't count ....
- ☞ I keep a spare tie (pair of tights) handy for emergencies ....

How would you describe your general appearance?
- ☞ Impeccably well-groomed ....
- ☞ Neat ....
- ☞ It depends on how much time I have ....

1 – Your dress sense must be in keeping with your professional image. Each sector of activity is associated with a certain style of dress. Our society sets great store by image so it's important to have the correct appearance to back up your professional capabilities. So, if you are pursuing a career in banking, your appearance must inspire confidence and precision: a subtle and classic elegance. You work in advertising? Seduction takes the upper hand here, a touch of originality is welcome as it suggests creative potential...

A client is reassured if the person he is dealing with conforms to the preconceived notion he has formed of them. Consequently, by abiding by the rules of the dress code, you are facilitating your commercial dealings. The way you are dressed tells its own story, and you will experience less difficulty in winning over a client and establishing your credibility.

2 – Wherever possible, adjust your appearance to suit your audience. We are not going into the techniques of NLP (Neurolinguistic Programming) here but this second rule is an obvious application of it. The more you resemble your client, the more his reservations about you weaken; thus a closeness in appearance will bring about an almost instant rapport: 'birds of a feather flock together!'

3 – Your general appearance can generate a feeling of warmth. Your smile and pleasant manner can help to create a positive climate. In the same manner, the way you are dressed may be interpreted as a reflection of your mood. Any normal person would prefer to converse with someone who's in a good mood, so it's up to you to ascertain what detail would brighten up your general appearance: a touch of colour to brighten up a black and grey outfit, a touch of lipstick to a face otherwise free of make-up, a handkerchief arranged in the breast pocket of an otherwise severe looking suit...

Having taken account of those points which work in your favour, be vigilant for those which could be classified as a turn-off:

- too much make-up or a shade of nail varnish that's too garish
- gaudy stockings
- 'loud' ties
- a conspicuous sex siren image – see-through tops or micro minis are out of place
- clothes in which you don't feel comfortable and which negatively influence your behaviour

YOUR APPEARANCE AND YOUR COMPANY

In the morning, do you base your choice of outfit on the type of people and the situations you expect to face during the course of the day?

☞ Yes, more often than not ....

☞ It depends, my priority is comfort in my choice of what to wear ....

☞ No, I never think about it ....

Have you adapted your style of dress to your current functions?

Yes ☐   No ☐   Don't know ☐

Compared to the dress code of your company, would you say that you are:

☞ More elegant ....

☞ More casual ....

☞ Normal ....

☞ You've never asked yourself that question ....

Do you ever have the impression that you adopt a role based on the people, places and situations that you encounter?

Yes ☐   No ☐   Sometimes ☐

Do you think it's normal practice to go beyond what your role implies if the image of the company is in question?

Yes ☐   No ☐

How would you react in the following situations?

☞ A visitor gets lost in the corridors of the company:
  - You spend five minutes setting him on the right path ....
  - You say hello and continue on your way ....
  - You ignore him ....

☞ Mr Murray's call is mistakenly put through to your line...
  - One moment please, I'm just connecting you with Mr Murray ....
  - No, this isn't Murray, you've made a mistake ....
  - I'll try and put you through to the telephonist ....

☞ You meet a disgruntled client, but you are not responsible for his upset, you tell him:
  - That's not my responsibility, I can't help you ....
  - It's the packaging department who have once again made a mess of the job ....
  - Can you explain the problem to me and I'll see what I can do ....
  - Go and see Mr So-and-So. ....

– jewellery which is too flashy...
The advice from our American counterparts is to be 'dressed for success'.

GENERAL ORGANIZATION

The organization of a company is usually regarded as the first yardstick of efficiency. It has a great deal of influence on the selling side of the business. Good organization, as you and your company will bear out, reassures your client on three levels:
– Your capacity to think ahead
– Your professional authority
– Your active involvement in all situations.

To reach these objectives requires a complete overhaul of the organizational systems . Ask yourself this question: 'How and when does the customer gain an insight into the quality of my organization?' Whatever range of replies you come up with you can be sure that two common denominators will come to the fore: speed and simplicity. To understand this a little better let's look at extremes:

SPEED ◆ DELAYS, WAITING
Each time a customer is made to wait, you can be sure it's your organizational skills that he will blame, and he will then question your ability to control delays, manage your timetable and manage your priorities...

SIMPLICITY ◆ COMPLEXITY, DIFFICULTY
The customer wants a smooth, easy route to the completion of his purchase, and not a path lined with pitfalls. So anything you can put at his disposal to facilitate his progress will be a step in the right direction. This will call directly on your powers of organization or, better still, of thinking ahead.

To keep your commercial affairs on a smooth and even keel demands absolute personal thoroughness and discipline, no matter what your level of responsibility. Here are a few pointers to help you:

Think ahead as far as possible and take pre-emptive action

☞ YOU ARE LEAVING A LITTLE LATE FOR AN APPOINTMENT?
– Have your secretary warn your client of the precise length of the delay. In this way you will appear to arrive punctually at the time announced.

THE ORGANIZATION AND YOU

A – For a meeting, are you most often:
1. Very early ....
2. Five minutes early ....
3. Just in time ....
4. A little late ....

B – A client has requested some paperwork. How swiftly, on average, would you reply?
1. The papers are sent out the same day ....
2. They are sent out within two days ....
3. They leave within the week ....
4. It depends on how busy we are ....
5. 'It takes its course' ....
6. You don't know, you pass on the instruction ....

C – You receive a client on the premises YES NO
1. Is the head of reception informed? ....
2. Has a conference room been reserved? ....
3. Do you have all the necessary papers to hand? ....

D – In the case of a delay in the delivery of a product:
1. You automatically think ahead and phone to warn him ....
2. You wait for him to show up before you offer any explanation ....
3. Once the sale is concluded it no longer concerns you and you are completely unaware of what happens afterwards ....

E – You need some precise information for your customer consultation (when exactly it can be delivered, availability, colour)
1. More often than not you know exactly who you have to contact in the company to get the information you need right away ....
2. You're not assured of a reply on the spot, so you note your client's question and promise to get back to him with a reply the following day (and you keep your promise) ....
3. You make five calls in front of your client without success ....

F – Do you present to your customer all the other people (at least indicating their names) that he will be dealing with at the various stages of the sale?
1. Automatically ....
2. Sometimes ....
3. Never ....
4. You have no idea what comes after your contribution to the process ....

☞ THERE WILL BE A LITTLE DELAY IN THE SERVICE THAT YOUR CUSTOMER IS EXPECTING
- Call him up two days before the fateful date for relaying the results and sell him the idea that the file contains such a wealth of detail that an extra few days will allow an in-depth study.

☞ A PRODUCT HAS BEEN DELIVERED INCOMPLETE
- Call your customer immediately to warn him. Be able to tell him when exactly (date) he will be in possession of the missing piece. If he's still not satisfied, appease him by offering a little compensatory extra.

Make out check lists

Nobody can claim to have a computer memory, so to avoid any last minute panic, get into the habit of making out check lists. In this way, listing in their entirety all the elements necessary to the smooth running of any event (a meeting with a customer, public speaking, presenting products, briefings...), will put your mind at rest and leave you free to do other things. With everything sewn up in advance there can be no possibility of a nasty surprise or unexpected circumstances arising in front of the client.

Inform your colleagues, regularly circulate:

- details of the identity and specifications of those you are dealing with, and the nature of customer files being processed, with your secretarial service
- specific requirements of certain clients, from the point of production to the after-sales section
- details of unusual conditions of payment negotiated between you and your client, with the accounts department

Etc.

PREPARATORY CHECK LIST
FOR ALL CUSTOMER VISITS TO THE COMPANY

☞ Security services warned to admit the visitor to the car park and to reception ....

☞ Identity and time of arrival of the visitor transmitted to reception ....

☞ A welcome planned ....

☞ Area of production (of demonstration) warned of a possible visit ....

☞ Directions for reaching the company and confirmation of the appointment
faxed to the visitor ....

☞ Conference room reserved from .... to ....

☞ Necessary documentation
Type: ....
Number: ....

☞ Refreshments/hot drinks lined up ....
Will be served by: ....

Before a meeting

☞ Audio-visual equipment necessary and available:
Overhead projector ....
Slide projector ....
Microphone ....
Video recorder ....

Your own instructions

GENERAL ORGANIZATION AND YOU		
Analysis of your replies from page 49		
QUESTIONS	INAPPROPRIATE REPLIES	REPLIES OF LITTLE COMMERCIAL WORTH
A	1/4	
B	4/5/6	3
D	2/3	
E	3	
F	4	

In the same way, inform those you have commercial dealings with:

- of your company's usual operational procedures;
- of the name and position, within the company, of those he could come into contact with through his dealings with you;
- of the procedures for confirming identity at reception if this applies;
- how the after-sales service operates.

And you personally need to counteract the effects of busy periods by setting up the sales aids already mentioned, (including those which you have added): standard check lists for each set of figures, whiteboard for noting information received and given, instruction cards...This thoroughness will help you to maintain an organized image in front of the client.

FASHION TRENDS

Are we speaking the same language?

The variety of fashions and trends doesn't prevent us from stereotyping individuals into categories. The salesperson has a particular interest in knowing about these categories since everything he learns about his client can lend weight to his abilities to persuade. The client, like all of us, is in the situation of constantly seeking approval, and he needs to feel that you share his value system or at least that set of values which he outwardly displays (by wearing coded dress signals for example).

We live in an era which is very fond of self-description and analysis. One useful guide is the excellent book by Christopher Golis, *Empathy Selling*, in which he analyses the sales prospect, under seven personality stereotypes: the mover, the ditherer, the artist, the politician, the engineer, the hustler and the normal. The sales proposal is adapted to the subtleties of the particular personality type you want.

DO YOU CAPITALIZE ON INVISIBLE SELLING? COMPLETE YOUR ASSESSMENT

What could you improve on in your sales area?

IN THE AREA OF	WHAT CAN YOU IMPROVE?	IS IT YOUR OWN DECISION? DOES IT HAVE TO BE NEGOTIATED? WITH WHOM?	TO BE CONDUCTED AS FROM... (SET YOUR DATES)
PREMISES AND SALES ENVIRONMENT			
CLEANLINESS/ HYGIENE			
APPEARANCE/ HYGIENE			
APPEARANCE/ BEHAVIOUR			
ORGANIZATION			
CORRESPONDENCE			
TRENDS IN FASHION/ TENDENCIES			

IMPROVING YOUR SELLING KNOW-HOW

Section 4
BUYERS = SELLERS

For far too long we have thought in terms of selling rather than buying, but the salesperson is constantly confronted with the best source of education in his field: his client and the latter's own observations about the process of buying. Buying consists of a succession of stages which everyone goes through regardless of the social background to, or the nature of the purchase.

Just how we eventually arrive at the act of buying, we shall examine in detail, as well as the manner in which the salesperson should behave at each stage of his client's buying fever; but beforehand we shall examine the different cycles and determine what buying code our customer adheres to.

THE TEN STAGES OF THE BUYING PROCESS

1 - Awareness of a need

This stage – awareness of a need – real or imagined, appears to arise spontaneously and without the customer really knowing why. Studies show that this feeling of desire is usually evoked by advertising which triggers the idea. The interviewee at this stage would never admit to being influenced by the mass media; is he even aware of it? The motive cited is either the denigration of the product in question: *'My car has had it'*, *'Our apartment is too small'*, or the express desire for something new which has been given a high profile promotion campaign on the street or in advertising: *'I've just got to have a pair of Reebok boots'*, *'I want a CD player.'*

TYPES OF BUYING

A. IMPULSE BUYING

He or she hasn't thought about it or displayed a conscious need; but all of a sudden they are struck by a craving whether for a tie seen in a shop window or a portable phone, a weekend in Paris or a particular nail varnish. Love at first sight is the same sort of thing. They've got to have it, and right away... All the salesperson should have to do is express the same enthusiasm for the item without trying to rationalize the client's sometimes incoherent motives. A state of grace to be taken full advantage of.

B. THE PURCHASE OF CONSUMER GOODS

It's less alluring, and is associated with dullness, routine and tedium. Even the client/salesperson duo don't really have any faith in it. In this context it's perceived much the same as flirting would be by a couple married for thirty years. Big investment is necessary in order to seduce the customer: an advertising campaign, attractive packaging and a novelty element.

C. THE PURCHASE OF CAPITAL EQUIPMENT

This is the one which requires most deliberation. This is the one which usually demands the biggest financial investment. It is to this type of purchase that we can apply the rules of conduct corresponding to 'psychological timing' and see how it influences the interested party.

THE BUYING PROCESS

The ten phases which count

1. Awareness of a need

2. Attention paid to the advertisements for the object of this need

3. Attention paid to those who possess the object of desire or similar products

4. Period of compulsive daydreaming

5. Back down to earth and meeting reality = Adapting the proposition to the means available

6. Process of pre-buying

7. The purchase

8. Justification of the purchase to the buyer's companion/ spouse/circle of friends

9. Novelty wears off, boredom sets in

10. Desire for renewing the process

The brand name, if it's effective (or more precisely if its advertising agency is), will manage to encapsulate this desire and assimilate it into the product; the marketing man's dream is to become a generic household name such as Kleenex, Walkman or Hoover.

Salespeople, relax, this is the phase where you have nothing to contribute! You remain in your office or your retail outlet powerless and peripheral to this assimilation phase. In culinary language we could say that the prospect is simmering!

2 – Attention paid to the advertisements for the object of this need

3 – Attention paid to those who possess the object of desire or similar products

The need becomes a conscious one. This is followed by a sudden interest in the advertising campaign concerning the product. It's at this point that, if the interested party were to be questioned, he would be capable of reconstituting all the publicity he has seen regarding the product. It is also at this juncture that word of mouth has its greatest influence. The person then proceeds to discover who among his friends, acquaintances and professional circle, possess the object of his desire. He painstakingly observes anything near and far which might resemble what he's looking for.

4 – Period of compulsive daydreaming

This stage is followed by the dream sequence. Not quite ready for the act of buying, our hero is content to dream. The notion of price isn't yet taken into account and the future owner of a Ford Fiesta is happy to indulge his fantasies of a Mercedes. No need for a salesperson until the time when hard facts impinge on his dream world where everything is attainable. Short but oh so sweet!

5 – Back down to earth and meeting reality = Adapting the proposition to the means available

It is at this stage that direct marketing has particular impact. The fantasy has run its course and frustration is now at its height; he doesn't believe in it any more! The future buyer now has his feet firmly back on the ground: he calculates, evaluates, compares. To anticipate his need for an adviser at this point would be a strategic asset. He is just realizing that he wants someone to talk to him about himself and the object of his dreams. The line of persuasion therefore has to focus on the suitability of the product, the means at his disposal and the need he wants to fulfil. To ask him questions would be the most appropriate technique; but now it's the salesperson's turn to stop dreaming; it doesn't strictly follow that the client is ready to buy. He has to be allowed to come and go as he pleases, without having too much pressure brought to bear on him. Let's release him, having whetted his appetite for the return visit.

6 – Process of pre-buying

The process of pre-buying is the next step. We're in the high season of comparisons. Come armed and ready to bargain for now it's time to prove your convictions, the future buyer is winding up his tour of the market. It's the moment when he is accumulating all the documentation possible. Get out your brochures, and be sure of yourself.

A good salesperson can thus shorten the cycle and conclude the sale. However, don't rush anything and certainly do not adopt an injured air if you hear those famous words, *'I want to think it over'*.

It's not a pretext or an escape valve. The modern consumer is an adult, he acquires his information and he wants to see in front of him an 'adviser'. He will not be at all favourably impressed by a smooth line of sales talk. He expects the salesperson to accommodate his needs. All this does not imply a passive salesperson for this is also the moment when the customer is most attentive to any 'extras' you propose (after-sales service, facilities, assistance...). These factors will contribute almost as much to the final decision as the arguments/products which he can evaluate on his own.

7 – The purchase

Refine your discourse, we have reached D-Day and may the best seller win! Go into labour with the client and be vigilant so that it is painless: modes of payment, reassurance, sincerity...

KNOW HOW TO CONCLUDE
Restrain yourself and don't exhibit feelings of triumph at having succeeded in making a sale. At all costs avoid saying *'You won't regret it'*...which immediately has the effect of giving the customer doubts about the decision he's just made.

8 – Justification of the purchase to buyer's companion/spouse/circle of friends

At last, the marriage has been consummated! Our contented beneficiary has made his choice; he is happy, but he still needs to justify himself: 'Have I done the right thing?'

In order to convince himself he is going to try out his personal line of persuasion and thereby be transformed into a salesperson. If you should have occasion to meet your customer at this stage, it's the right time to 'over-argue', something you couldn't permit yourself to do at the moment of purchase. Now you're free to praise, no need to show impartiality!

This would be the perfect moment, if possible, to play the role of 'patron'. Proud of his new toy, Mr Client has only one idea in his head, to enrol disciples. He is ready to found a village, consisting entirely of his own relatives, around the detached house he has just bought or make all his friends buy a pc just like the one which now occupies his every waking hour, not to mention the credit card which makes him a member of a club for which he is ready to become a recruiting officer. If during this short space of time someone were to suggest that his circle of friends/relatives too should benefit from a venture into the world of consumerism, he would readily agree to do something about it.

It would show sensitivity to this attitude if you accompanied this proposition by a letter, affirming the interest you have in him as customer; but this is only appropriate, of course, if the buyer is the purchaser of important capital equipment or services, etc.

9 – The novelty wears off and boredom sets in

'Thus everything passes, thus everything palls'. The purchase is already a thing of the past and may be completely forgotten. This not being the case, it's the time for the breakdown, missing parts and after-sales service. The touch of human tenderness which identified the selling stage does not mark this period, and as for the salesperson, he has usually disappeared from the scene. However, this is an interesting period and difficult to manage because it can in fact stretch from 18 months to 10 years! Here, 'Customer Services' or 'Consumer Departments' come into their own, for only influential, well-established organizations can offer the client any degree of satisfaction at this stage.

10 – Desire to start all over again

The wheels of a new cycle are set in motion. The desire for a fresh start sets in. The significant question is this – did you have any influence on this new decision to buy? A well-organized customer file constitutes the basis for a possible relaunch, but avoid immoderate eagerness! Who hasn't fallen victim to the following situation:

The contented owner of a luxury saloon after a hefty financial output, is still satisfied with it two years after the purchase date. However, such an investment could only be justified – and he was convinced of this at the time of buying – if he kept the thing for a period of five years. And there should be no doubts on that score, should there, given the quality of such a vehicle? Yet it so happens that regularly, every three months, the over-zealous salesperson calls him up to enquire: '...*Still happy,*

Mr Thingamyjig?' The tone lets you know that if this is the case, then it's an unusual one. And the second time: '*Tell me Mr Thingamyjig, would you not be considering changing it one of these days?*'; it's just that he worries you see, the poor thing. 'He's had a bit of bother with this model... no, no he's not telling you this to give cause for concern, it's just that the new version is so much better...'

By the third call the buyer is fed up and no wonder!

It's a pity that capitalizing on this customer follow-up should have exactly the opposite effect:

– breeding suspicion about the quality of the brand
– implicit cover-up of the association between value for money, duration...
– no concern shown for the client's motivations
– harassment – even a little is too much!

THE RENEWAL OF 'SERVICE' OFFER

1 – a courtesy call making a POSITIVE proposition to the client, (free offer of a brakes check-up or some other little service perhaps not worth very much financially but proof of continuing interest)

2 – afterwards, prepare a questionnaire with the aim of establishing the client's frame of mind and his intention to change

3 – ask for authorization and the opportunity to re-establish contact at such and such a period corresponding to the client's intentions

4 – conclusion: Don't denigrate what you have just sold but do make preparations for the future: 'It's a bit soon but in six months time would you like to receive information about our new models?'

ADVERTISING AND RENEWAL

Do you know how to capitalize on advertising and the desire for renewal?

1 – In your professional environment, how could you be more effective during stage 10?

2 – Are you completely up-to-date with the advertising campaigns in progress?

3 – Do you know what the campaign's objectives are and what kind of desire they awaken?

4 – Do you use them as points of reference when dealing with a client?

5 – Who can help you if your replies are inadequate?

PERSONAL NOTES

Section 5
AND THE SELLING GOES ON

So that's it, you've made your sale; you are now at stage 7, buying, described in the previous chapter. Don't allow yourself to get carried away by the excitement, justified though it is, of acquiring a brand new customer. It is really only after this first sale that the true commercial relationship begins.

It is in maintaining customer loyalty that the real profit of this first contact will materialize. Knowing how to hold on to a customer and in particular how to capitalize on his potential in an intelligent fashion, represents for a company, not just a means of guaranteeing its place in the market but also of increasing its status among its competitors. It now depends more than ever on the quality of the after-sales service to boost the package on offer, in the face of greater demands by the consumer for consideration and that 'something extra'. This type of demand transcends the actual service or product sold. It calls for a sense of creativity in dressing up the product to give it prestige. This will induce in the customer a sense of enjoying a slightly privileged position. Each time a customer makes a complaint, looks for further information or generally makes themselves known in any way, it is a now or never moment to develop a lasting and therefore profitable relationship with him. The nature of this 'relationship' selling is often the antithesis of a short-term procedure, as it implies:

1 – the establishment of special systems: customer services, databanks...

2 – a commercial spirit in which the selling ideal is taken on board by the whole company from production to marketing

3 – a new type of mentality: you must 'think client'. Thinking client implies making contact with him as often as possible after the purchase but without repeating the old mistakes of the customer harassment policy.

The unfortunate victims of the old policy hadn't even finished paying for their first purchase when they were already being approached once, twice, three times . . . with a new proposition.

Follow-up procedures and further campaigning depend, for their impact, on catching the customer at the right time with the right message. To control an after-sales relationship of this kind requires a permanent capacity for anticipating the client's needs. Needs which may be either real or psychological depending on the type of repeat situation.

To this we can add peripheral needs such as maintenance, supplementary products, financial arrangements, etc. More difficult to control, the financing is associated with the initial investigation as it's at the moment of purchase that you should put together a file on the nature of subsequent propositions of possible interest to the client.

The two categories of need described here (recurring and peripheral) will permit relaunches which are ultimately more directly commercial. It is a matter of increasing the 'lifetime value' of a client by leading him to consume once again.

THE CONDITIONS OF SUCCESS

1 – The time factor

You have discovered how to calculate precisely the right moment to reappear on the scene, but there is no strict rule governing this matter other than that dictated by the customer himself.

This supposes on your part:
– an appreciation of the length of time necessary to awaken a new need;
– an ability to calculate the timing of a second approach based on the client's estimated financial means. In general, returning from holidays, end of year or the aftermath of Christmas are not usually synonymous with intense bouts of consumer fever!

2 – The clear-sightedness of your proposition

In an ideal situation, your approach would result in the customer announcing:
'You couldn't have called at a better time!' A targeted proposition is appreciated by the client as it proves to him that you have a genuine knowledge of and interest in his business.

FOLLOW-UP METHODS

1 – THE 'COURTESY' FOLLOW-UP

This can consist of a phone call a week or two following the sale.

OBJECTIVE: *'Is everything going well?'*

This action presents two important advantages:

a) demonstration of an interest in the client not directly associated with the act of buying;

b) discovery at a very early stage of any possible signs of disappointment; by anticipating them you can defuse any risk of problems later.

The courtesy follow-up is unfortunately a little-practised strategy; it is usually accepted that silence is a good sign and an unhappy client will soon make himself known. Furthermore, surveys on the subject have shown that only the extemely satisfied or the extremely dissatisfied indicated as much to the salespeople.

What happens to the silent majority?

The figures speak for themselves.

ONE PROBLEM FOR EVERY FOUR PURCHASES

70 PER CENT OF CONSUMERS DON'T COMPLAIN:

– because they don't know who to contact

– because they think it's not worth the effort

– because they think that the company involved won't do anything about it

OF THIS SILENT 70 PER CENT:

– 63 per cent change their brand

– *90 per cent express their dissatisfaction to ten people they know.*

Of the 30 per cent who react and receive a satisfactory response to their complaint: 68 per cent become loyal customers.

---

3 – The 'service' dimension of your follow-up

Anticipating the client's need and addressing it even before he's had time to take the initiative himself is associated more with a SERVICE than with an act of sale. The key to success in a commercial follow-up: not to give the impression of selling but of offering a service. For example, informing a subscriber that after the next two issues of his favourite magazine, he is likely to receive no more; why not alert a client to the arrival of a new addition to his word processing package? And what a relief it would be for mothers if their doctor would take the initiative and systematically notify them of the need for booster vaccinations for their children!

The direct commercial objective is only a link in the chain. The ground is more favourable and fertile if it has been prepared in advance. This preparation is made for the most part through the means of contact which could be termed 'complimentary'.

S mile

E xplain the offer

R eact quickly

V alidify the product's value

I nform

C reate loyalty

E ngender the relationship

FOLLOW-UP METHODS

2 – FOLLOW-UP ALSO KNOWN AS 'REASSURANCE'

It's a second form of general approach (that is to say without any direct sales objective) which allows us to call on the client and cultivate a commercial relationship with him. This type of follow-up usually comes about in the situation where the customer experiences and expresses dissatisfaction (delay in delivery, breakdown, errors in billing...). The aim is to ensure that everything has been settled according to his expectations and that you are available should the need arise. The consequences are similar to those which arise in the previous case, the context merely serves to increase their intensity. In fact it is in these situations that the customer is more intent than ever and he is especially more vulnerable in the face of:
  - the unequivocal reaction of his friends and acquaintances who don't hesitate to cast doubt on the wisdom of his choice: 'We warned you', 'You've been had', 'You didn't negotiate enough', 'You should have been expecting this'...
  - his own doubts, which he won't hesitate to extend from the particular product to the entire brand name, deciding not to use it again.

3 – FOLLOW-UP TO RETAIN THE CUSTOMER

It is standard practice, but nonetheless worth remembering that it is essential to hold on to the customer. This type of follow-up maintains a presence in the client's consciousness. A commendable service as certain types of clientele are overlooked, as in the case of the 'small fry' clients. In the interests of profit, commercial departments concentrate more on the big accounts, so a section of the clientele, sometimes significant, find themselves ignored and look elsewhere.

CUSTOMER SERVICES

What services are offered to the customer through this means?

1 – Proximity and accessibility.

2 – Competence: in an ideal situation, Customer Services would be equipped to deal with any query coming from the client.

3 – It must be efficient: there's no point in encouraging customers to get in touch if you are ill-equipped to deal with the demand.

4 – The service must do more than handle complaints.

5 – After-sales service is only one aspect of customer services.

6 – The customer should feel he belongs to a 'club' and that you are fostering a real relationship arising from the fact that he is a customer.

THE TASKS OF CUSTOMER SERVICES

A – To INFORM *(to reply to the queries of the customer is the surest way of attracting him to buy again);* Depending on the capacity of the service to manage large quantities of information (existence or not of a databank), the response will be whole or incomplete.

In the event of it being impossible for the service to deal with customers' enquiries in detail, it should instead act as an Information Centre. This means that it should be sufficiently familiar with the entire working mechanism of the company to be able to direct the customer to someone competent to deal with these queries. Thus the service becomes a kind of intermediary between company and client.

This 'function' is particularly desirable in two cases:

1 –Where the size of the business, the complexity and number of items on offer are such that a wide range of expert knowledge must be called on to handle enquiries.

2 –Where the image of the business (for different reasons) renders it inaccessible.

ADDRESSED TO THE BOSS

☞ Mark out the lines between customer dissatisfaction and the internal reasons for this discontent. The link between the two falls into the domain of your competence. It's a basic connection which you have to sort out yourself.

☞ Find out why customers like your company; this is often more important than asking why rejection and ignorance of it is so great. Surveys always record the reasons for complaints.

☞ Insist on objectives and directives based on factors appreciated by the consumer. Make sure they appear in all instructions concerning your products and services.

☞ Get involved: the head of a company should not be content just to talk about added value or even to define it exactly, but also to contribute actively to it.
For example: At Disneyworld, a high ranking executive who notices a cigarette butt on the ground, bends down to pick it up himself.
The value of training by example?
The Managing Director of 'Dupond' in France phones personally and on a regular basis people who have written letters of complaint.

☞ Be wary of using company jargon; sometimes it almost requires a professional translator to decipher it.

☞ Have a healthy respect for other languages. How do companies with a high international profile dare to publish such inaccurate translations of instructions for use of their products? (And this is the case for at least 30 per cent of them!) Established faith and credibility in a company are undermined by a lack of accuracy or errors found in basic matters.

No 'rag bag' help line

Opening the door to clients can lead to an increase in unforeseen demand.

Limiting a consumer service to the role of information centre carries with it the risk of not being able to channel the nature of questions asked.

The services offered by a direct consumer number must therefore be clearly specified to clients.

B – MANAGING COMPLAINTS

Particularly well-developed consumer services can go so far as to anticipate certain types of complaint. Studies show that a high proportion of breakdowns in new equipment can be explained by either a careless reading of the instructions for use or a lack of them altogether. The manuals are very often off-putting and can discourage the consumer. Replaced by a help line which can explain step by step the first operation of a new product to its owner, such a service is a real preventative measure which considerably limits the subsequent cost paid out on guarantees. Widely practised in the United States, this kind of assistance is still at the embryo stage elsewhere. American companies never hesitate to go beyond the call of duty to win over a client and keep him loyal.

C – ADVICE, A SALES ARGUMENT

Advice is becoming more and more the aim of the phone numbers printed on packaging. And, in fact, if one is mulling over a question, goods in hand, whether to put this one or that into the shopping trolley, then the deciding factor could well be the presence of a freefone number. This number guarantees a reply to any queries.

This notion of advice is already implicit in numbers of products or services. Clearly set out, this advice can explain the full benefits offered by customer services.

Let's take a few examples:

BEAUTY PRODUCTS
ADVICE ON BEAUTY AND APPEARANCE

FOOD
TIPS ON HEALTH/RECIPES

READY TO WEAR
ADVICE ON LOOKING AFTER THE FABRIC

CAPITAL EQUIPMENT
INSTRUCTIONS FOR USE AND MAINTENANCE

WINTER SPORTS RESORT
ADVICE ON ACTIVITIES ACCORDING TO THE DEPTH OF SNOW, WEATHER FORECAST, CROWDS...

WALLPAPER, CARPETING
TIPS ON INTERIOR DECORATION

MAKE YOUR CUSTOMER SERVICE A SUCCESS

1 – BY PROMOTING IT
The customer can't have recourse to it unless he knows that it exists... Stating the obvious still has its uses!

2 – BY DEFINING ITS AIM CLEARLY AND EXPLICITLY
This is necessery both internally and externally; everybody should know exactly what to expect.

3 – BY EXPLOITING ITS ADVANTAGES TO THE FULL
The value of a customer service goes beyond the immediate reinforcement of one's position *vis-à-vis* the competition. Any direct contact with the client, and especially at his own instigation, is an opportunity to be grasped.

EXAMINATION OF CONSCIENCE

☞ Do you offer a form of assistance to your clients?

☞ Are you in contact with customer services?

☞ Have you given it the personal attention necessary to improve it (or contributed to its existence)?

☞ Do you confuse the idea of a mundane after-sales service with a customer service?

One unhappy customer, ten bad echoes.

Advantages

1 – The ability to play the role of adviser is associated with a high level of knowledge and competence and this, in itself, inspires confidence.

2 – The impression of getting more value for money: product + SERVICE cheapens the offers of competitors without a helpline 'number'.

3 – Guarantee of sincerity: 'Since the brand name answers for itself it must have nothing to hide!'

Sopad Nestlé recently moved from third to second position in the French market (behind Gerber) in babyfood products, by developing these kinds of quality 'services'. Among them, 'Hello, Dietetic Nestlé' is a freefone number printed on the packaging of all their products and in their advertising campaigns. This number permits mothers to question the four dieticians manning the lines, ten hours a day and six days a week, on the nutritional needs of their babies. The high quality of the reception and advice given is so appreciated by consumers that 500 of them write to thank Nestlé spontaneously each year.

ACTIVE COMMUNICATION

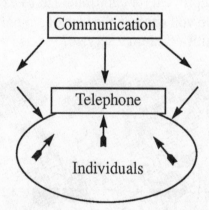

RECEPTION OF CUSTOMER CALLS

YOUR RESPONSE TO THE CONSUMER

☞ Can each of your clients easily get in touch with your company? How are requests for information treated? ....

....

☞ Is the running of the complaints department centralized? Who is in charge of it? How does the follow-up procedure operate? ....

....

☞ What 'EXTRAS' (service or advice) do you or could you offer your clients? In what ways? ....

....

☞ Who benefits from the quantity of information supplied by 'after-sales' contact? ....

....

☞ If you had to give an assessment of the running of the 'after-sales follow-up' directed at your clients, what would be its:
– principal strengths? ....
– principal weaknesses? ....

☞ What improvements are conceivable:
– in the short term? ....
– in the medium term? ....

☞ What would be the main difficulties to overcome?
Concerning you: ....
Concerning your professional environment (colleagues, structures, work procedures...) ....

....

☞ How do you intend to proceed? ....

....

WHAT OTHER BENEFITS CAN BE GAINED FROM A CONSUMER SECTION?

A customer service may be considered successful once it becomes a centre of profit in itself. Two types of profit indeed may be drawn from this.

1. A direct profit

Direct repercussions arising from the existence of a customer service on sales. We have already elaborated on its ability to win new clients and make them loyal to the company.

At the same time we should underline the possibility of achieving additional sales. The success factor rests then with the speedy reactions and commercial sensitivity of the telesalesperson. Here we discover the true definition of a 'SITTING SALES FORCE'. The approach to the client should be dealt with in two stages:

– first and most important, satisfaction with the object of the call;
– in the second place, if point 1 has been resolved and only if the client is favourably disposed to the idea, proposals for supplementary products or services.

An atmosphere of confidence is generated naturally since the customer is in control of the situation, and the 'sitting' salesperson can tap into the neutrality of the situation which has not been set up primarily for selling. The line of persuasion can thus be all the more convincing.

Let's analyse the following example:

SUBSCRIBER: *'I'm really very disappointed with the quality of your service. The last two editions not only arrived late but also in very bad condition, completely torn up.'*

SALESPERSON FOR CUSTOMER SERVICES: *'Thank you very much for bringing this to my attention, this information will enable us to be careful about this for the next batch. What numbers in particular presented problems?'*

SUBSCRIBER: *'The last two editions.'*

SALESPERSON FOR CUSTOMER SERVICES: *'I shall immediately send you two further copies in perfect condition to compensate for this incident. Apart from that, are you still satisfied with our journal? Did you read the article on...?'*

SUBSCRIBER: *'Yes, it was very interesting, I especially liked...'*

SALESPERSON FOR CUSTOMER SERVICES: *'But tell me, I see Mr Murray, that your subscription is coming to an end?'*

FREE GIFTS –
DO THEY HELP MAKE A SALE?

What does it involve, the free gift and 'little bonus' destined for the client? If these fall naturally within the framework of the after-sales service, then they should be handled with tact and courtesy. 'Offering know-how' is an art in itself.

Correlation between the value of the gift and the objective to be reached

A token offering of little value may strike the intended recipient as a belittling gesture and consequently tarnish his perception of the company's image.

On the other hand, something of too great a value might lead him to suspect the company of trying to buy him off. His suspicions being aroused, subsequent propositions by the company may appear suspect to him.

Correlation between the nature of the gift and the customer profile

In the same way as dress codes exist according to the sector of activity or superiority of position occupied, so there exists a system of regulations governing the matter of 'free gifts'. Respecting these regulations makes it possible to achieve a threefold objective:

1 – 'to give pleasure', by responding to tastes which have been investigated beforehand
2 – to surprise and demonstrate a level of initiative (image bonus point for the company)
3 – promotion, by displaying, in the choice of a certain range of items, an understanding of the status of the intended beneficiaries.

SUBSCRIBER: *'I don't know, I think it's up sometime in December...'*

SALESPERSON FOR CUSTOMER SERVICES: *'It's a good thing you rang me today as I've just received the subscription forms . . .would you like us to fill out a renewal form? And just as a bonus I'll set aside for you our special free gift offer usually reserved for new customers.'*

SUBSCRIBER: *'That's a good idea...'*

SALESPERSON FOR CUSTOMER SERVICES: *'And of course I'll send you out those two missing issues... I'll list you as of today among our subscribers for 199., in that way you won't suffer a break in your subscription.*

'If it would suit you, I can take a note of your credit card number straight away; that would speed up matters and it's one less thing for you to worry about!'

SUBSCRIBER: *'Okay, that's fine by me!'*

The selling reflex is not, however, a gift from the gods. It involves instilling a SENSITIVITY and MOTIVATING and INFORMING your colleagues in consumer services. This function should not be viewed as strictly administrative, those concerned should all be regarded as salespeople 'in the field', at the core of the company's commercial policy. However, it is of vital importance to remember that this channel of selling remains an auxiliary service whose PRINCIPAL AIM IS ASSISTANCE, information and advice.

On no account should the consumer feel he is being 'trapped'.

2 – Indirect profit from consumer services: gathering of information.

Telephone calls, letters or electronic messages received from customers represent a mine of information. A shrewd use of this spontaneous recovery of data can reduce the number of market studies carried out.

CONSUMER SPECIAL

95% ➤ LOYAL if you were pleasant and solved their problem.

54% ➤ will remain CLIENTS if they were looked after (even if their problem remained unsolved).

19% ➤ 'COMPLACENT' because they were listened to even if their problem went unsolved.

Here are the principal applications:

☞ EXTENSION OF THE CUSTOMER DATABASE

Apart from updating standard details (addresses, socio-demographic grouping, position held within a firm, etc), this allows us to obtain further information about each customer in a more personalized manner. This may include information about the client's tastes, his view of proceedings, his habits of frequenting sales outlets. Current computer methods offer possibilities of control and identification, leading to classification and planning.

☞ REINFORCEMENT OF NEGOTIATING POWER WITH SUPPLIERS

A regular evaluation of complaints permits an investigation of the technical imperfections which crop up most frequently. Such an analysis, categorized according to product, enables a rapid identification of the source of the trouble. If a cog in your own company is to blame, the results will prove invaluable for the establishment or reinforcement of a 'quality control programme'. If the weak link concerns the performance of a supplier, then here the client is your spokesman via the motives expressed in the complaint.

☞ ORIENTATION OF TRAINING PROJECTS

The same analysis as that described in the previous paragraph, but applied to the employees of the company rather than the products, could bring to light any deficiencies in terms of service. When lodging complaints about the behaviour of a company representative, clients have no hesitation in describing in detail the exact reason for discontent: discourteous reception, incomplete or misleading information given, promises not adhered to... So much information to be exploited by a head of training.

Reasons for dissatisfaction most often expressed may then be incorporated into courses/training programmes based on relevant themes. Training projects nowadays should be modelled on customer demands and not just on the wishes of the employees themselves. This is an efficient method of ensuring the effects of training at one time: programmes built around real situations and experience in the field become 'TRAINING IN ACTION'. Their operational dimension distinguishes them from more theoretical assignments where the trainee has difficulty in finding the link between what he experiences on a daily basis and the content of the presentations.

☞ EDUCATING THE STAFF ON THE IMPORTANCE OF THE CLIENT

It is absolutely essential that everyone, no matter what their function in the company (worker, accountant or Managing Director) keeps in mind that the ultimate aim of that function is to satisfy the client. Circulating letters of complaint reinforcing this concept of a client-led organization, to certain sections of the company who are not in direct contact with the public, is much more effective than vague speeches about motivation.

Some companies have been able to create one source of education, using information drawn from these complaints. In particular, the consumer services section of a large furnishing company transmits extracts from complaints verbatim to the Managing Director on a regular basis. This man, it would seem, doesn't sleep at night, but his sensitivity to his clients' welfare is exemplary.

Commercial follow-up brings with it radical change at the core of the company. It demands a complete synergy of all modes of operation. Territories, hitherto segregated and autonomous: after-sales service, production, marketing or management of human resources, are reconciled to working together. The 'selling spirit' spreads gradually and through it the company is endowed with a new feeling of responsibility. By putting the spotlight on the client, objectives become more concrete and motivating for the company as a whole.

Section 6
PROFESSION: SALESPERSON

If the art of selling lies in conquering a primitive desire for victory over the client, the salesperson should also avoid an inverse and restrictive inclination towards transforming himself into a vague public relations figure. To sell is above all to 'seek out' the buyer. The procedure exists and it is a dynamic commercial offensive, unlike after-sales care which is simply the maintenance of an already existing relationship.

To seek out the client is to accept a confrontation, to prepare to measure up to him. You must descend into the arena and no technique or device will take away the dreaded moment when you must take a step towards the client. The techniques for making an approach differ according to whether the sales target is an individual or in a commercial context, business to business.

In the former instance there exists a foil between the client and the sales-person: the sales premises. Boutiques, department stores, supermarkets and all kinds of shops, develop a signposting system which replaces the baited hook of the salesperson. The client is attracted by the look of the place and enters of his own free will. Promotions and low pricing have taken over the function of an invitation to the customer and the appeal of a sign is a direct generator of traffic. Maximizing these effects raises the potential for business for the salesperson who immediately takes up the challenge, after this first step.

WHAT MAKES THE CLIENT ENTER?

1. Precision is a sure winner

If Monoprix in France distances itself from the concept of being a 'popular store', in order to present itself as the 'store at the heart of your town', if Lenscrafters want to be perceived as makers of glasses in '1 hour', this is not by chance. The customer is attracted by the distinction and so commercial arguments have been transferred from the spiel of the salesperson to the store signs. This gesture evidently appeals more to the customer who needs less time to stop and take in what's being offered. So the message must be easy to grasp and address a need more concerned with the method of consumption than the product itself.

2. Location

The success of a particular site can often rest on a single detail: a free parking area, or a stop sign or traffic lights in an inspired position opposite the shop . . .
Also, the site is a determining and strategic factor. It's a question of combining economic criteria with good old common-sense factors.

3. The allure of the premises

The sales premises must present all the exterior signs of 'consumer pleasure', the client buys first with his eyes. A nondescript shop window, an unclear shop sign, unremarkable decor, blaring background music, are all major turn-offs. New consumer trends are leading to an increase in appreciation through the senses: everything must look beautiful, smell beautiful and be good value. Thus the look of the premises must adapt itself accordingly. The current trend is for harmony and a return to the natural look. Forms are rounded and supple, colours are deep, materials choice and lighting as natural as possible. The store is a show-case with its goods on display. The client no longer enters to ask a salesperson for a product he needs but to lose himself in an atmosphere which favours buying, if possible on impulse, if not, through seduction.
40 brands of toothpaste, 191 brands of canned vegetables, 55,000 boutiques . . . here is an abundance which calls into play factors of choice other than those inherent in the products.

THE PREMISES CHECK-UP

☞ Are there any 'pace-setters' in your neighbourhood, in other words, strikingly attractive shop signs, open when people are on their way to work or late in the evenings?..

....

☞ Is there a possibility of a pedestrianized zone?...

....

☞ Is access to the store practical? Are there parking facilities (preferably free)? Is the area often subject to traffic jams?

☞ Does its location encourage passers-by to stop (layout of pavement area)?

....

☞ A consideration which may be unusual but is still important: is the site 'positive'? Verify historically that it is not 'cursed'. There are in existence certain addresses which have seen the successive failure of all their inhabitants! ....

....

☞ Are any significant urban planning works forecast?
– Pedestrian zones, notable road works, modifications to the traffic system.

....

☞ Is there any connection between the retail or commercial site and its vicinity? (Kitchen or decorating companies sited near established affluent housing estates, little pockets of antique dealers in Islington or near Portobello Road...) ....

....

☞ How could you attract the attention of the passers-by?...

....

THE QUALITIES OF THE SALESPERSON

Once the conditions are reconciled, our salesperson comes on the scene. He should display the following qualities:

1. Patience

Do *not* descend on this desirable client as soon as he enters the place. You should respect this first contact between store and customer without, of course, feigning complete absence. Know how to capitalize on the seductive powers of the premises. Allow his desire to grow and give him time to make his first tour of the display.

2. Know how to advise

There he's hesitated... The correct approach is not to interrupt in order to describe, you must talk about the product as the buyer would: from the point of view of a consumer. It's often said that salespeople do not know the product, that they are merely trained in systems. Customers think longingly of individual shopkeepers – the real professionals who knew their goods intimately (bookseller, butcher, beautician...).

Somebody selling sports shoes has to know what types of shoe are suitable for different sports, the sales assistant in a music shop has to know all about the latest bands, the motorbike seller must know his Hondas from his Harley Davidsons, etc. This understanding and even intimate knowledge of the product reinforces the image of the salesperson as adviser. If two products seem to satisfy the client in a rational sense (value for money, correct technical specifications...) then the deciding factor might well be supplied by the seller's expertise.

3. Skill

The modern consumer profile is markedly ageing: the number of people over 60 in the EC has risen by 50 per cent in the last 30 years to 68.6 million. This characteristic implies in part a demand for quality and service. The retail manager or independent shopkeeper cannot be defined exclusively as a salesperson, involved as he is with his products as much as with the satisfaction of his customers. There exists a subtle difference between these two positions, of shopkeeper and salesperson.

ARE YOU A SALESPERSON?

NO	YES
– You're out of luck! – You should have come three weeks ago... – We're out of it. (negative triumph)	– I don't have that model at the moment, but if you like I could have it for you in ... days.
– What's the problem?	– Can I help you?
– Can't you see anything you like? – Nothing suits?	– Have you seen the latest model X from the Italian designer?
– I'd have to go and check in the stockroom and I don't have the time.	– If you could just wait a moment and I'll check the stock, we may still have one or two left.
– I've already told you...	– As I pointed out...
– You should have come sooner! It's gone within two days...	– As you can imagine, this article has proved very popular and I don't have any left at the moment.
– We won't get another delivery for two months! Call back.	– I'll take a note of your phone number and notify you when the delivery comes in.
– That's not my responsibility.	– I'll take care of it.
– That's for you to decide.	– To help you decide, can I just ask you if...
– Is that it?	– Have you seen our umbrellas? They're funny aren't they?
– We've had too many problems, we don't do alterations anymore.	– I can recommend an excellent alteration service very near here.
– Normally it should be ready by Tuesday...	– It will be ready on Wednesday.
– Ah no, we don't accept that credit card.	– We do accept credit cards or, of course, you could write a cheque.

Once the customer has entered the shop, the desire to please and satisfy that customer should influence the saleperson's selling techniques. The client knows this and subconsciously he seeks out the 'boss' who embodies this commercial attitude.

The salesperson often appears to be interested only in closing a sale. His personal financial interest is all too obvious in the process. Certain methods of remuneration consisting of commission (small) and a percentage linked to the turnover figures, explain why such aspects as quality and communication are sacrificed to the race for time which represents money.

HOW TO RECONCILE SALES INITIATIVE AND RESPECT FOR THE CONSUMER

– By introducing to the recruitment criteria, the ability of a candidate to communicate with the client (level of general knowledge, personal interests, feeling for others, natural curiosity...).

– By drawing on modern management aids in running the shop (computers, optical character reader...) to capitalize on data collected (breakdown of turnover figures, customer profiles...) and save on the salesperson's time.

– Use documentation or a training programme to promote a courtesy policy company wide which will personalize your brand name.

– Insist on your sales personnel sticking to the recommended behavioural policy in operation on the premises. By doing this you can form a list of all unbusinesslike attitudes and behaviour present in the company and educate each salesperson on the errors to avoid.

WHO IS AFRAID TO SELL?

The symptoms of the fear of selling are widespread. Identify them in the following statements:

☞ *'Well, we're certainly not going to talk business now are we?'*
                In that case, why are we here?

☞ *'I don't want to appear as though I'm giving you a sales line!'*
                That's just what I'm expecting.

☞ *'I never have my card on me.'*
                Are you afraid somebody might find you again?

☞ *'It's not in my interests to sell you that.'*
                And how is it in my interests to buy it from you?

☞ *'I doubt if we'll be able to do that.'*
                We don't just do anything.

☞ *'I look after the commercial side of things, not sales.'*
                So what does the commercial side of things involve?

☞ *'Could you go directly to a sales assistant with that?'*
                You dare to address me?
                In any case, the next time round it'll be the competition!

The misunderstood company pride

'We don't explore prospects, clients come to us unsolicited.'
'We only do business with a select dozen companies.'
'You know, we deal with a very specialized market.'
                (... you could never be one of our clients.)
'We only attack the big markets.'
                (... who do you think you are?)
'We could do it but we're not interested in it.'
                (... and our interests are more important than yours!)
'We reserve that for export only.'
                (... so go and look elsewhere...)

BUSINESS TO BUSINESS

Traders or salespeople in business-to-business dealings are right on the front line. It is necessary to launch an offensive. A worldwide reputation and a top brand image will usually open the doors of potential clients. However, when they will not, the prospects need to be softened up by advertising campaigns, mail shots, cold calling or telesales.

Business-to-business transactions take place between experienced people: buyers who work with a specification and know exactly what they want and how much they can pay, and sellers who have to take account of this. The impulse and emotion involved in personal purchases do not come into play here.

Business buyers tend to be loyal to existing suppliers because their strengths and failings are known; a new company might be able to match the required price but needs a very clever strategy to supplant the current source. A psychological approach is called for.

Loyalty to an existing supplier is an indicator that the buyer might well be as loyal to your company if he could be persuaded to change.

Ask the buyer if he remembers *when* he changed suppliers before. How long ago was it? There have been many changes in products and their uses since then and he might find it worth while to let you run through them with him, and see how his firm could benefit.

Ask the buyer if he remembers *why* he changed suppliers. Find a way to apply his reason to the current situation and use it to persuade him to give you a trial order, or to accept a trial delivery on a sale or return basis. You are playing for big stakes so do not rush these delicate negotiations.

There is no good Managing Director who does not apply himself to the task of motivating and mobilizing his commercial team, which includes the entire complement of his workers. Selling to businesses requires business knowledge and product knowledge. The salesperson should be familiar with the competition – its products, prices and methods of selling. A truly professional approach is called for, powered by enthusiasm. Everyone in the company can be considered as part of the sales team.

HOW TO HELP THE SALESPERSON

1. Work in synergy with the means developed by the company

While these means can in no way replace the personal initiative of the sales-person, he must have his own perception of them and be able to incorporate them into the selling procedure.

- By MAXIMIZING the profitability of various actions *(a mailing for example only has maximum effect if follow-up action is taken ten days after distribution and, conversely, a phone call is facilitated if the interviewee has been approached in advance).*
- By PROMOTING the status of the salesperson. He is the representative of the company. As such he should be privy to all the secrets from on high, but very often it is the consumer who is more 'in the know' and is capable of telling the salesperson a thing or two about his own company: new publicity campaigns, press coverage, public demonstrations, presence or participation in trade fairs...

2. Linking the approach to reality

Cold calling, in other words, contacting a person you've never met under any circumstances, requires the formulation of some pretext, which may in certain cases be provided by the service itself if it possesses a sufficiently novel aspect. But it is often necessary to draw on your creative powers to develop a pretext which will justify and substantiate your approach. Keeping up to date with economic and professional publications could be a source of help. Linking your sales approach to current events is an extra assurance of success.

The clearer the objectives and the stronger the pride in belonging, the more powerful the motivation will be. To make the personnel proud of their company must therefore be the primary aim of the director, which implies a management of the synergy between internal and external communication:

- Advertising campaigns which have been discussed in advance with the sales personnel.
- Regular press coverage reporting the success of the company.
- Media exposure of the head of the company (in small doses!).
- Sponsorship or patronage in spheres of interest to the personnel.
- Reinforcement of business ethics and reputable commercial practices.
- A share in the success of the company for the personnel.
- A positive sales message, whatever the circumstances...

The motivation of the sales personnel is the FORCE which will allow them to confront prospects and clients.

All the peripheral activities shouldn't make us forget the transition to the act of selling itself. The seductive ambience of the sales premises leads to an exchange between the salesperson and potential buyer. The daily lot of the salesperson is to make his approach armed solely with his energy and desire to persuade.

The good salesperson is someone who understands the buyer's point of view. By revealing the client's hidden desires, the salesperson will know which of his offerings will answer a particular need and be able to present it in the most flattering light. Once the client realizes how sympathetic the salesperson is, he will want to maintain the relationship and buy again in the future.

The psychological make-up of the salesperson is no secret: difficult to handle, sensitive and touchy, manic depressive, that's him.

AH! THEY THINK THEY'RE DOING BUSINESS WITH IDIOTS !!

FIVE POSITIVE CONSEQUENCES OF CRISIS

1. A stronger reaction from businesses in the face of market needs

At times of crisis, the consumer wants good value for money, and will seek it out. Purchasing power is concentrated on essential items rather than impulse buys, and quality items are preferred for their lasting power. So sellers must adapt their offerings to a changed market.

2. Giving priority to talent

It's the time to make yourself appreciated.

☞ The demands of the consumer are directed at quality and service?
The answer lies with the competence and professionalism of the men and women who make up the workforce.

3. Increasing involvement of personnel in their company

☞ Team spirit is revived in times of crisis, so much the better if this is accompanied by a closing of the gap between personnel and consumers. They have a common aim – to trade to their mutual benefit.

4. Clearer communication

☞ The formal, grandiose language of earlier decades must go. Communications from a company must be clear and its directives straightforward.

5. A system of internal promotion

☞ Placing priority on talent results in a dedicated workforce which knows that rewards are based on COMPETENCE rather than COMPLACENCY.

And how could he be otherwise, because he's on the line from first thing in the morning until the time when others are heaving sighs of relief as they tidy things away before going home.

The euphoria of a successful sale is short-lived, and the constant pressure to do better – often to achieve self-imposed targets – becomes increasingly wearing on the nerves. Perpetually increased turnover is the law of the economic jungle, and sales people are the hunters who stalk and capture the prey. These problems are shared throughout an organization, from the bottom to the top.

The boss of a particularly large advertising agency, responsible for many famous campaigns, and recognized as one of the leading lights in his field... confesses to feelings of acute anxiety whenever faced with the prospect of calling a potential client! There is always a moment when we must take a deep breath and take the plunge. For some it's the very first step that's the most difficult, others balk at the prospect of announcing a price or negotiating a discount, many dread the final moment of the signature... In these circumstances, the salesperson should exude an air of confidence and understanding.

PROSPECTING WITH COMPOSURE

One of the reasons behind a 'fear of selling' is the fear of disturbing or bothering people. The salesperson must now convince himself of three things:

1. His unique competence and approach in promoting the product or service are in themselves an advantage. No two sales people will sell the same product in the same way. What the prospective client found uninteresting at Duffy's, he may find fundamental at Murray's.
2. Interpersonal contact is of the utmost importance and adds another dimension to the product: the client does not buy the product for its own sake but for what it becomes through the performance of the salesperson.
3. In the professional area, no matter what the function of the person contacted may be, his skills contribute to a perpetual learning process which must be constantly renewed and updated. In this way, meeting a salesperson or supplier can be seen as a form of free service on offer.

THE VALUES WHICH SELL

The ethic	Behaviour	Consequences for sales
– The notion of a fair price	– Not to knock the competition. – Not to sell based on the consumer's desire to buy but on the genuine value of the offer.	– Value for money.
– Satisfaction of a job well done	– Dignified conduct conditioned by belief in the quality of the product on offer.	
– Openness	– Honesty of employees. – An end to backhanders and 'commissions'. – An end to schemers/dirty business.	– Re-establishing confidence. – The return of respect for 'intermediaries', when previously just the mention of these caused immediate flight.
– Respect	Is it contagious? A value which in itself sums up the concept of correct behaviour.	– A salesperson who is both respected and respectful creates an ideal sales climate.

Through his performance, the salesperson should strengthen the image of his profession. So let's stop viewing the commercial relationship as one containing an inherent imbalance with the salesperson making constant demands. This psychological obstacle overcome, it remains only for the salesperson's personality to influence his approach to a prospective client. Two distinct groups can be identified here: the 'hunters' and the 'breeders'. One isn't a better performer than the other, comparable results are obtained by each type while their approach and understanding of the client are entirely different.

This divergence means they complement one another very effectively if each approach is properly carried out.

THE HUNTER only receives a buzz from the departure to conquer fresh fields. The 'Don Juan' of negotiation, he employs all his energies to seduce and win over his client. This objective attained and his mission fulfilled in his own mind, he can pass on to the next prospect... The focal point for the hunter is the 'run up' to the sale. The essence of selling for him is represented by the confrontation aspect and the subtle game of persuasion he engages in. All other aspects bore him. He only surpasses himself when the game is particularly difficult. This selling cossack is most often an extrovert, self-confident charmer. He feels at ease in flexible systems, fast moving situations, even crises, and atmospheres charged with emotion. His impact on a system is particularly dynamic: he can carry along the sales figures as well as the customers. His principal weaknesses lie in his difficulty in dealing with anything in the long term. Impulsive, he lives for the here and now. Thus, a client who takes a long time deciding is abandoned, and the after-sales relationship completely neglected. Instinct first and foremost and with bouts of success or bouts of bad luck!

THE BREEDER – if he doesn't match the brilliance of the hunter – makes up the deficit in the long term. His skills find their outlet in the notion of time. He takes time to establish strategies and study his prospects. His reactions take longer, his interventions are more calculated, his preferred selling territory is that of the hot prospect, the freshly acquired clients (state market, administrative sector). He likes nothing more than after-sales follow-up and feels he is still capable of selling something more.

EXAMINATION OF CONSCIENCE

What lack in ethics is implicitly associated with your profession?

....

Could you be instrumental in their improvement?...

....

Which?...

....

How?..

....

What decisions could you make in this context?..

....

What flaws in professional behaviour damage your commercial results?

....

Who benefits from them? ....

....

How and with whom can you resolve certain aspects?

....

EXAMINATION OF CONSCIENCE

A. Take the role of client and describe the type of product or service you would like in your professional sector.

B. You are the president of your company for just one day. What would you do to increase the company's productivity rate?

C. If you were your Director, what would you have to say about your capacities as salesperson or colleague?

There's nobody better placed than he to manage the continuing relationship with the client. His commercial energies are spent less in the direction of conquest than in maintaining customer loyalty. Reassuring and constant, he is the one who will compile an individual file for each of his clientele and establish long-lasting and profitable relationships. Anchor man of the sales team, he watches over the basic running of the system while the hunter seeks to enrich it.

If it is essential for a commercial supervisor to establish a sales team based on the individual skills and similarities of each salesperson, it is also desirable for him to recognize and make use of both hunters and breeders. Without corresponding to these extreme stereotypes, you can still discover a dominant tendency in each salesperson and adapt it to a suitable role in the team. This will make the task of integration and gaining results that much easier.

The hunter
The breeder

FINAL POINT

Selling is now a much more organized activity. The different industry sectors have their own watchdog bodies to enforce a code of practice or customers' charter, and in some cases the codes are enforceable through government legislation.

Large corporations have come to adopt a more caring response towards those with whom they are in contact: customers, employers, shareholders, suppliers and their local communities. Their reformed attitudes are expressed in corporate mission statements. The entire organization is mobilized to 'sell' itself to its various publics and such back-up can only help the salesperson in the front line – making the sales to make the profits which give corporate success. Sales policy is based on a fair deal for the consumer – a quality product at a reasonable price.

Salespeople are themselves more equipped to do their job. Excellent training programmes are available throughout the country, and many firms offer courses in house. Specialist instruction is obviously necessary for the selling of complicated equipment such as high technology items in the medical, manufacturing and computing field. The high flyers who work at such levels reap considerable rewards.

FURTHER READING FROM KOGAN PAGE

Empathy Selling, Christopher G Golis, 1992

How to Perfect Your Selling Skills, Pat Weymes, 1990

Inspired Selling, J T Auer, 1991

Know Your Customers, Jay Curry, 1992

Sales Training Basics, Elwood N Chapman, 1988

Sell Your Way to the Top!, Peter Thomson, 1993

Selling Professionally, Rebecca L Morgan, 1991

Selling to Win, Richard Denny, 1989

Talk is Cheap, Godfrey Harris and Gregrey Harris, 1992

The 25 Most Common Sales Mistakes… and How to Avoid Them, Stephan
    Schiffman, 1991

25 Successful Sales Techniques, Stephan Schiffman, 1992